As We Knew Him

Painting of Dom Basil by Robert Lange

Reflections on M. Basil Pennington

❧As We❧ Knew Him

Compiled and Edited by Michael Moran and Ann Overton

PARACLETE PRESS

BREWSTER, MASSACHUSETTS

As We Knew Him: Reflections on M. Basil Pennington

2008 First Printing

Copyright © 2008 by Michael T. Moran

ISBN: 978-1-55725-539-6

Library of Congress Cataloging-in-Publication Data
As we knew him : reflections on M. Basil Pennington / edited by Michael
Moran and Ann Overton.
    p. cm.
Includes bibliographical references.
ISBN-13: 978-1-55725-539-6
1. Pennington, M. Basil. I. Moran, Michael. II. Overton, Ann.
BX4705.P423A88 2008
271'.12502—dc22   2007050463

10 9 8 7 6 5 4 3 2 1

Published by Paraclete Press
Brewster, Massachusetts
www.paracletepress.com
Printed in the United States of America

Dedicated
to
Basil Pennington
A faithful monk and priest,
a spiritual presence and teacher to many,
and a friend to all

In the year 2007,
the 50th anniversary of
his ordination to the priesthood.

"I am a person who sits each day at the feet of my Lord and listens to him in his inspired word.

I am a person who each day sits in silent meditation allowing the Lord to refresh me."

M. Basil Pennington, OCSO

"The journey to God follows many roads. So let each person take to the end and with no turning back the way that was first chosen."

Saint John Cassian

"Examine closely what sort of being you are. Know your nature—that your body is mortal, but your soul, immortal; that our life has two denotations, so to speak: one relating to the flesh, and this life is quickly over, the other referring to the soul, life without limit. Give heed to thyself—cling not to the mortal as if it were eternal; distain not that which is eternal as if it were temporal."

Saint Basil the Great

Contents

Preface   xiii
Michael Moran and Ann Overton

Part One
∾ PRIEST AND MONK

St. Joseph's Abbey   3
Spencer, Massachusetts, 1951–2005
The Beginning and the End
Matthew Flynn, OCSO

The Ava Years   12
1986–89 and 2000
Mark Scott, OCSO

REFLECTION   18
Karol O'Connor, OSB

Our Lady of Joy   19
1991–98
Theophane Young, OCSO

Our Lady of the Holy Spirit   27
2000–2002
Elias Marechal, OCSO, and
Francis Michael Stiteler, OCSO

REFLECTION   31
Thomas Keating, OCSO

Part Two
～ FAMILY MAN

Uncle Bob   35
Megan Lange

Pennington Family History and Myth   38
M. Basil Pennington, OCSO

The Penningtons and Their Religious
   Vocations through the Centuries   50
Jasper Pennington

REFLECTION   57
Cynthia Pennington

Part Three
～ MAN OF PRAYER

Reflections on Monastic Meanings in
   the Twenty-first Century   61
Laurence Freeman, OSB

Apostle to the Laity   73
Martha F. Krieg

The Beginning of Centering Prayer   79
Armand Proulx

Personal Encounter with Basil Pennington   85
Grace Padilla

REFLECTION   95
Gerry O'Rourke

Centering Prayer and Salesian Spirituality:
   Connections   97
Lewis S. Fiorelli, OSFS

REFLECTION 102
Stephen J. Boccuzzi

Part Four
DREAMER AND CREATOR
Free to Love: The Dreamer and the Realist 107
E. Glenn Hinson

How Basil Pennington Came to Kalamazoo 120
John Sommerfeldt

REFLECTION 126
Werner Erhard

A Life Lived Abundantly 127
Ann Overton

Part Five
HUMAN BEING AND FRIEND
Welcoming the Stranger 137
Arnold Mark Belzer

Lessons in Love 141
Franck Perrier

REFLECTION 147
Erik P. Goldschmidt

Surrendered to Love:
  The Challenge of Living Prayer 150
David G. Benner

Set Us Free, O God: Basil and Dance 156
Bruce Stewart

REFLECTION   164
Robert Goldschmidt

Fully Present   165
Casy Padilla

For What Am I Thankful?   169
Michael Moran

About the Contributors   179

Appendix

~BASIL'S THREE CORE TEACHINGS
AND SPIRITUAL PRACTICES

Guidelines for Centering Prayer   187
M. Basil Pennington, OCSO

Guidelines for *Lectio Divina*   188
M. Basil Pennington, OCSO

Guidelines for Preparing a Rule of Life   189
M. Basil Pennington, OCSO

Chronology   191

Glossary   195

Bibliography of Books
Written by M. Basil Pennington, OCSO
Compiled by Martha F. Krieg   199

Bibliography of Scholarly Books
Written by M. Basil Pennington, OCSO
Compiled by Martha F. Krieg   207

In the foreword to his book *Called: New Thinking on Christian Vocation,* Basil wrote, "I write because I love, and I want to share what I have received." This book is an expression of love for the man and the monk, Basil Pennington. Each of us knew him in our own way, and all the contributors here happily share some small portion of what we received from him in such abundance.

Also included here is a piece written by Basil originally for one of his nieces, telling the daughter of his brother Dale all about the Pennington family. (See the chapter, "Pennington Family History and Myth," by M. Basil Pennington, ocso, in Part Two.) It offers a fascinating look into Basil's view of family, the Roman Catholic Church, as well as his views on life and death, which were eventually made real in his own living and in his dying in 2005.

For our part as editors, Michael worked diligently to gather reminiscences from those who knew Basil at different times in his life and in different contexts. Not everyone he asked could find the time in their schedules to say yes to his request, and a few old friends and colleagues could not be contacted. For these omissions, we apologize. Ann edited each contribution with an ear tuned to the well-told story and an eye turned to eliminating repetition. Where we have fallen short in our efforts, we ask for your forgiveness.

For those of us who knew him, Basil Pennington was an unforgettable presence and someone who made an enormous difference in our lives. If you knew Father Basil, we are confident you will encounter his presence again in these pages. For those of you who did not know him, we hope through these stories you, too, can share in the difference he made.

One of the truest expressions of love is joy. It has been a labor of love to bring this book to life, and it is our joy to share with you Basil Pennington as we knew and loved him.

Faithfully,
Michael Moran
Ann Overton

Part One

PRIEST AND MONK

St. Joseph's Abbey
Spencer, Massachusetts

———•———

1951–2005
The Beginning and the End

Matthew Flynn, OCSO

On the feast of St. Benedict, March 21, 1950, a tragic fire destroyed the Cistercian Abbey of Our Lady of the Valley, in Valley Falls, Rhode Island. The community of 150 monks relocated to Spencer, Massachusetts, in December 1950, changed its name to St. Joseph's Abbey, and resumed the full monastic life on a dairy farm in the rolling hills of central Massachusetts. Two months later, in February 1951, Robert Pennington visited this monastic community, convinced that this was where God wished him to be.

Robert entered St. Joseph's on June 18, 1951. He was given the name, Frater (Latin for brother) Basil. He received the novice's habit after one month as a postulant. Six months later, I entered the monastery and joined Frater Basil as a novice. Our Choir Novitiate consisted of twenty-five men. Father Hilarion Summers was the novice master. Father Hilarion had a unique style of directing novices, making sure that they left the novitiate with their false ego broken and seriously wounded. He called the process "cracking the nut," allowing one to be transformed into Christ. In the morning, Father Hilarion would summon a novice, identify one of his predominant faults, and reduce him almost to tears. By day's end, he would check to see how the novice was coping. Father was happiest when he saw that your pain led you into the church and that you spent time pleading for help before Jesus. His mission was accomplished if, through prayer, you found peace. He would then assure you that God loved you and that in prayer you would find his love and peace.

Frater Basil's many talents were immediately manifested. He possessed detailed knowledge of all church minutiae. He was proficient in Latin, enabling him to master the Divine Office. His physical stature was an asset in all work situations, as he stood six foot, five inches and weighed about 250 pounds. Basil excelled in everything he did, save one—he was tone-deaf.

As a novice, Basil's inability to sing was a major problem. During this time, the community was comprised of two groups: choir monks and lay brothers. The choir monks were priests whose main duty was to sing the full Divine Office five hours daily. They were also obligated to perform five hours of manual labor. The lay brothers worked eight hours and were responsible for the monastery's maintenance.

Five hours in church singing the liturgy was challenging. Basil, however, was unaware that he was tone-deaf and did not understand why he was advised to sing softly. I was assigned to the stall next to Basil in choir. When the novices went to the middle of the church and stood around in a large choir, I stood closest to the book with Basil directly behind me. At the peak of his fervor, Basil sang with all his heart and emotions, and the power of his full and off-key voice forcefully descended upon me.

Basil was large in every way, and his fervor was no exception. He devoted all his energy to community prayer, liturgy, and manual labor. Novices were allotted three or four hours each day for private prayer and *lectio divina*. He used this and any additional free time in quiet prayer, kneeling before the Blessed Sacrament. God does not give the grace of contemplation in the same way and degree to everybody. Basil received this grace abundantly. Without it, one could not spend countless hours kneeling motionless in prayer. Most of us would be fidgeting and restless. God was generous to Basil. I am sure those hours of prayer were where Basil first experienced the peace of contemplative prayer and were the impetus for his many seminars and retreats on Centering Prayer.

My first job as a novice was working with Basil in the sacristy, where he demonstrated his organizational skills as the novice in charge of preparing the daily private Masses said by each monk-priest. There was a Mass Crypt with twelve altars, and vestments for the next morning's Mass were laid out on each altar. The wine cruets were prepared and placed in the refrigerator. Basil was also responsible for setting out vestments for the visiting priests who resided in the guesthouse and celebrated Mass after the monastic priests had offered theirs.

Frater Basil also spent many hours working on the farm. At harvest time, farm work was a major occupation for the novices. During haying season, one novice would pick up each hay bale and heave it onto a flatbed trailer, where the stacker, frequently Frater Basil, would pick it up and stack it in an orderly and compact fashion. This was essential, because the tractor then pulled the trailer a good distance to the barn with a dozen more novices perched upon the haystack. At the barn, the bales would be restacked. Basil's strength was a major asset for most farm-related jobs. He completed his tasks swiftly, challenging fellow novices to keep pace.

He did have one major mishap. He often drove the tractor that took the manure spreader onto the fields. There was a power take-off (a type of rotating drive shaft) on the back of the tractor that connected with the spreader. The take-off powered the machinery in the spreader that propelled the manure. The spinning take-off was a true hazard. In those days, all monks wore long, heavy, denim work smocks. One day, Basil jumped off the rear of the tractor and his smock became entangled in the machinery. His smock was ripped from his body by the take-off, and he was severely injured. He was fortunate to survive this accident. His misfortune was the impetus for the discontinuation of work smocks and the introduction of coveralls. Eventually, blue jeans became the work habit.

The groundbreaking for our permanent buildings began in 1952. On March 19, we processed up the hill to the spot where the high altar would stand in the new church. The tremendous work of building this large complex of cloisters would now begin in earnest. All the stones that constitute the outside of the buildings were gathered from the stone walls that surround all the fields on the property. Crews of novices would go with a tractor and flatbed, and select stones that had a face and flat bottom. Far more stones were gathered than were chosen for use. A construction company was supervising the work and a group of the strongest lay brothers joined the union, working for the contractor. The rest of us did side jobs, like collecting stones and going to the railroad freight yard to collect the bricks for the interior of all the rooms as they arrived from a factory in the Midwest. Basil and two choir novices assisted the builders. We celebrated Mass in the new church, eighteen months later, on August 15, 1953.

1953 was a special year for Basil. He had survived the novitiate and in May 1953 was preparing himself for simple profession. The question of his tone deafness, however, had to be addressed. Our abbot, Dom Edmund Futterer, was concerned. As soon as the community had arrived in Spencer, Dom Edmund determined to perfect the choir and requested expert assistance from the great Abbey of St. Peter's of Solesmes, France, to train the monks in this highly developed method of chant. Dom Edmund, who had perfect pitch, wanted our expertise in chant to be second nature to us. He envisioned our being able to sink into the Divine Presence as our souls rested in God and our voices praised God in perfect peace. Ideally, we would be free of any distractions or worries about tempo and pitch.

Understandably then, Dom Edmund had reservations about Basil's vocation to the choir. Since the abbot, unfortunately, could not become well acquainted with all twenty-five novices, he had to rely on the Novice Master's recommendation of worthiness to make profession. (A novice who could not complete the studies for the priesthood—if, for example, he were tone-deaf—could be asked to join the lay brothers.)

Father Hilarion summoned me into his office and asked what I thought about Frater Basil and whether I would be willing to see the abbot and plead Basil's cause. I told Dom Edmund that Basil had a great devotion to prayer and that he was the most generous person in the novitiate. Dom Edmund thanked me and subsequently Basil made his simple profession on the feast day of his most beloved saint, the mother of Mary and grandmother of Jesus, St. Anne, on July 26, 1953. Basil was ecstatic.

During the fall after Basil's profession, the Vatican issued a decree that all professors of theology must possess a Roman degree to qualify as teachers of students pursuing the priesthood. We had professors who had been teaching for years, but none had degrees from Rome. So Dom Edmund hired a Dominican professor to live in our guest house and teach theology. This was the beginning of Basil's illustrious career as a scholar.

Our Dominican professor immediately recognized Frater Basil as one of his brightest students. After completion of his studies, Basil was ordained to the priesthood, December 21, 1957. Dom Edmund wanted to have his own priests as professors. This necessitated sending them to Rome for their degrees. Father Basil was one of the first to be sent. He set sail in 1958, navigating the cheapest way possible on an old freighter, headed first for Naples and then up to Rome. He studied at the Angelicum, living at the Trappist Generalate. He returned home with an SDL in theology (equivalent to a master's degree). A year later, he returned to Rome for studies, acquiring a degree in canon law. He was awarded each of these degrees, summa cum laude.

Father Basil returned to Spencer in 1962, as professor of canon law and spirituality. He was chosen as a member of the Law Commission of the Order in 1967, following the Second Vatican Council, at a time when the order was beginning to rewrite its constitution. Father Basil put all of his energy, generosity, and intelligence into this work. I served on several monastic councils with him, and it was here that he demonstrated his genius. He was always most objective, and his grasp of the situation was so comprehensive that he could synthesize all that was said and recite it back with accuracy. He always was the last to speak, and we all listened with a certain amount of awe.

In 1968, Basil initiated what I consider to be his greatest achievement, the translation of the Cistercian Fathers. In May of that year, the American Region of Cistercian Superiors accepted the plans for *Cistercian Publications*. The first volumes were published eight months later. Others will have much to say about his work in writing and publishing books. I remember where it all began, at his little desk in the professor's room, off the main cloister.

In addition to his many accomplishments, Basil successfully combined these activities with living the daily life of a monk. One of his positions was as night infirmarian. A fellow monk, Father Raymond, was an aged man who awakened in the middle of the night, needing someone to assist him to the bathroom.

Father Basil would sit in the chapel all night, waiting for Father Raymond's page, which he would immediately answer and, with his big arms, assist Father Raymond as needed. When Father Gerard was dying from cancer, he would wait for Father Basil to come to his aid. With one great swoop of energy, Father Basil was able to lift him, while others could neaten his bed. No one else could do this and cause as little pain as Father Basil.

Father Basil had a particular devotion to the dying. When a brother was nearing death, Father Basil would be at his bedside day and night, holding his hand or just being there, praying quietly. As one brother said to me, "I sure hope someone like Father Basil will be with me when it is my time."

Father Basil's prayerful disposition proved invaluable for the establishment of Centering Prayer. He assisted Abbot Thomas Keating and Father William Menninger in instituting Centering Prayer retreats and workshops. These were initially held in our guesthouse. There were times when the guesthouse was closed to all but those interested in Centering Prayer. As one of the retreat masters, I was not always sympathetic. At that time, I found it difficult to refuse a room to someone whom I thought God, in his providence, was sending us and was in need of our help. I now see that God had a greater plan. Centering Prayer has extended across the globe, providing guidance in the experience of prayer.

In the 1970s, Basil began to travel, but no matter how far away, he mailed cards to each of us, commemorating our birthdays, as well as the anniversaries of our profession and ordination. He never forgot us. When he returned home, he was delighted to give a big bear hug to each of his fellow brothers. On Sunday during his time at home, he would visit with me, and we would share the Sacrament. By now, you must know that I admired Basil as a religious and as a dear friend.

One place where we miss Father Basil is in the attic of the machine shop, where he constructed a Byzantine Chapel. This was before ecumenism became so widespread. The chapel was a rustic, open-beam barn where he placed an altar and a screen decorated with icons to divide off the sanctuary as is necessary for Eastern Liturgy. I think his introduction to the Eastern Church was at the Russicum in Rome where students loved to go for the beautiful liturgies. Basil eventually went to Greece and stayed at Mt. Athos for several months. Many years later, they still remember Basil on that holy mountain. How could Basil not make an impression with his physical presence—his white beard, piercing eyes, warm smile, and large stature?

When word came that Basil was in a terrible car accident, I was devastated. I visited him daily at the University of Massachusetts Medical Center in Worcester. He was in good cheer during our first visits. He befriended several members of the medical team who cared for him. However, his health rapidly deteriorated, requiring multiple surgeries and being placed on a ventilator. Communicating with him became quite challenging.

In the final weeks of his life, he became withdrawn and refused visitors. He was frustrated with the status of his health and did not want others to see him in this weakened state. During the last days of his life, the medical staff noted additional hemorrhaging and suggested further surgeries. Father Basil communicated to the physician that he adamantly refused any additional procedures and that he "had had enough." The attending physician informed Abbot Damian of Basil's decision. The abbot asked me to accompany him to Father Basil's bedside. Upon our arrival, the ventilator was disconnected. Over the next six hours, the abbot and I sat with him, holding his hand and praying. Father Basil, however, was completely unresponsive. You could sense his painful course was nearing its end.

Back home, the monks were chanting second vespers for the solemnity of the Sacred Heart of Jesus, June 3, 2005. During this time, Father Basil took his final breath. This feast was one of Father Basil's favorite devotions. His presence will be sorely missed in the community, but his memories remain. May he rest in peace.

The Ava Years

—•—

1986–89 and 2000

Mark Scott, OCSO

Father Basil was overflowing. He was overflowing with gifts of nature and grace. Like any overflow, his could not be contained—not by superiors, and not by the boundaries of ordinary Trappist-Cistercian life, a life to which Basil was dedicated with heart and soul.

Once during Father Basil's first sojourn at Assumption Abbey (1986–89), he and another monk attended the annual meeting of the Squires Volunteer Fire Department near the abbey. Like a true resident of the Ozarks, Father Basil wore his denim bib overalls. During the meeting, one of the ladies brought out a plate of cookies she had made. She handed the platter to "the Reverend" so he could help himself and then pass the platter on to the next person. Father Basil helped himself—again and again. Oblivious to the fact that there was only one platter, and that its contents were intended to be shared all around, Father Basil in the course of the meeting appreciatively devoured all the cookies.

Another time on Father Basil's first Ash Wednesday as *superior ad nutum* (an appointed, interim superior; *ad nutum* is Latin for "at the nod") of Ava, he gave the homily before the distribution of ashes. It was a participatory homily. In the center of the choir, a stainless steel salad bowl from the kitchen had been placed on a wooden stand. In the bowl were some oily rags. They had been lit, so they were smoldering. Each monk came to deposit a slip of paper he had prepared in the bowl. On the paper were his sins, his faults, or something he wanted his Lent to help burn away and purify. As the papers accumulated on the oily rags in the salad bowl, the thin steel became hotter and hotter. Soon it was glowing. So was Father Basil, who, unaware of the impending conflagration, or simply unconcerned by it, continued with his Ash Wednesday homily.

Father Theodore, meanwhile, ever the practical monk, bowed, went out, and came back. Up the sleeves of his cowl, he had concealed a small fire extinguisher that he very shortly unveiled and opened up on the flaming salad bowl. Father Basil continued his homily, gesturing for Ted to sit down, or calm down. But the flames broke out again, and Father Ted emptied the little red canister, putting the flames out the second time. After Mass, a monk spotted Father Basil outside, his chin in his hand, contemplating with prayerful yet chastened humility the black bowl with its still-soldering rags.

Another time, the bishop of the diocese, John Leibrecht, who admired Father Basil greatly, invited him to speak at a gathering following solemn vespers in the cathedral. During the psalms, Father Basil fell asleep, and the fact could not be hidden. Hardly anything about Father Basil could be hidden. Sometimes this was in spite of his intentions, but more often than not, hiding was not of uppermost interest to Father Basil and his way in the world.

How could Assumption Abbey, a small, isolated abbey in the Ozarks of Missouri, with nothing at all approaching the glamour and sophistication of the abbey at Spencer that Basil had entered and grew as a monk in, confine him? It couldn't. No place could. But he did confine himself—twice—and suffered the constraint while serving without calculation.

The invitation to come to Assumption Abbey came in 1986 from then superior Dom Flavian Burns. The idea was for Father Basil to foster vocations. It was thought he could do this, not just because of his growing renown as a spiritual master, but also because of his experience with Tabor House, a vocation initiative that Basil had started at Spencer. Basil could also foster vocations by hosting retreats and going on the speaking circuit to make Ava better known.

Basil devoted his characteristic energy to the task. He also was decidedly instrumental in the abbey's inspired choice of making fruitcakes as a new industry after their concrete block plant had been closed down.

In 1988, after Father Basil had been at Ava for two years and was known by the community, there was an abbatial election. Father Basil certainly must have expected to be elected, but it was not to be. Late in the afternoon of the day of the election, the new abbot went to Father Basil's room. Father Basil was sitting on the edge of his bed in the darkening unlit cell, his disappointment evident but private.

Typically, Father Basil rebounded, just as St. Paul always did after failure and humiliations. He continued at Ava for another year. He kept up his vocation ministry. While no vocations he attracted to Ava persevered here, the Heartland Monastic Vocation Directors's Meeting that Father Basil started continues to take place each winter at Ava, and is now in its twentieth year. He also expanded his speaking engagements outside the abbey and was away more than he was at home that year.

After Father Basil's first stint here at Ava, he had a similar but longer mission at Our Lady of Joy on Lantao Island in Hong Kong harbor. As he had at Ava, Father Basil devoted his talents to promoting Cistercian life at that refugee monastery. Lantao also served as a base from which Father Basil visited the Philippines and other areas in Asia where the order is present. During Father Basil's time at Lantao, that monastery rose to the rank of abbey and Father Clement Kong was elected abbot. For the rest of his life, Father Basil would tell with justifiable pride how his years of work in China had been completed with the blessing of the first Chinese abbot in history.

In the late 1990s, Father Basil returned to Spencer and started adjusting to the idea of retirement. This was when his second, but shorter, stint at Ava began. As the year 1999 came to an end, Assumption Abbey was again without a superior. The abbot had resigned, and the community did not feel prepared to elect a new abbot right away. Consulting the community and searching around for candidates who were both capable and available to serve as temporary superior at Ava, the Father Immediate, Dom Brendan Freeman, Abbot of New Melleray, settled on Father Basil.

The appointment was not without some controversy (which, in the context of Ava, is never anything more than mild). Dom Brendan had consulted all the members of the community, old-timers and newcomers alike. The old-timers, who had known Basil during his first tour of duty a dozen years earlier, felt that he was, as one of them says, "too big" for this small, remote community. More seriously, some felt that Father Basil's way of operating lacked adequate reflection and consultation (or, as another puts it, Father Basil was "a bull in a China shop"). On the other hand, the newcomers who knew Father Basil only through his books and reputation thought it would be "nothing short of cool" to have Father Basil as their superior.

When Father Basil got the news of his appointment, his leg was still in a cast from a broken ankle. "Coming back to Assumption Abbey is indeed a return," he said in the abbey newsletter. "I knew the seniors well and loved them very much. The call to serve again is a very special grace." It could only have been Providence and divine poetry that Father Basil began his service as *superior ad nutum* at Ava on Valentine's Day, February 14, 2000. He quipped that he was "a Valentine for the Community!"

With his energy and talents, Father Basil began organizing committees to plan the second stage of a building program at Ava. He located architects and, with the community's wholehearted backing, continued to raise funds for the project. With a vision as big as God's, Father Basil wrote, "When the calendar turns to the year 3000, monks will be here at Assumption Abbey, continuing to pray for the friends who built this abbey, and for their heirs and progeny, for the church of Missouri and the whole universal Church, for all the family of God." He also directed his attention to vocational recruitment and initial formation, and invited Father Mark Scott (me), a monk from the Abbey of New Clairvaux in Vina, California, to join the community of Ava temporarily to help him with this.

Just six months after undertaking his ministry as *superior ad nutum* of Ava, the monks of Assumption Abbey received the news that Father Basil had been elected abbot at the Abbey of the Holy Spirit in Conyers, Georgia. This news was completely unexpected to the monks but not entirely unexpected to Father Basil.

Just prior to the election at Conyers, Father Basil had gone to visit there. As he explained to the Ava community at the time, he had been asked to help the community of Conyers in its discernment process leading up to the election. In fact, though, Father Basil knew he was one in a small pool of candidates singled out by the Conyers community as possible future abbots. When Father Basil went to Conyers then, it was at the invitation of the Georgia monks who were gathering the candidates together to present them to the community's scrutiny.

Understandably, there were various reactions at Ava to the news that Father Basil had accepted the election at Conyers.

There was confusion, there was resentment, and there was anger. Admittedly, on the part of some, there was relief. There was also uncertainty, since once again the question of leadership of Ava was back on the table. But the monks of Ava accepted Father Basil's assurance that he had prayed and consulted his spiritual director before finally accepting the election at Conyers as God's will for him.

Not unlike St. Paul, Father Basil had a self-promoting drive. He recognized this and tried to channel it in a Christ-like way. Now and again, as everyone who knew him recognized, the driven-persona Basil would break out and reveal itself. He also had a childlike devotion to our Lady, and he explained that his patron saint was not Basil the Great of Caesarea, but Basil the Fool.

What kept Father Basil on track, with such diverse drives and gifts? He may have given us the answer in one of his conferences for the monks of Ava. He told us that as a young monk he was struck by the passage in John's Gospel where Jesus tells his disciples, "I no longer call you servants, but friends." Father Basil was so impressed by this call to become a friend of Jesus, that for the rest of his life he used this as the material of *lectio divina*. His insight into our Lord's covenant relationship with his disciples seems to have been Father Basil's true center.

Perhaps Jesus confirmed Father Basil's personal spirituality by calling him to himself on the Feast of the Sacred Heart. One Ava monk, commenting on Father Basil's life among us, recalled what a provincial had said when asked what it was like to be the superior of a famous Dominican priest. He replied, "It was like leading a lion on a string, but the string never broke." Lion, bull, or gentle dove, Father Basil's heart was love.

REFLECTION

Karol O'Connor, OSB

When I hear the name Basil Pennington mentioned in monastic circles, a warmth encompasses my heart and I am drawn back almost thirty years to when I was a novice here at Kylemore Abbey, the monastic home of the Benedictine Order of nuns in Ireland. On one of the free afternoons when Father Basil was visiting with us, he asked me if I would like to climb to the statue of the Sacred Heart that overlooks our abbey. I jumped at the opportunity because I liked Father Basil from the moment we met. He was totally "over the top" and had a sort of aura that seemed to change everyone and everything he touched—truly Christ-like. He was wild, he was happy, he laughed a lot, he connected with everybody, and when he spoke, it was as if nothing else existed but his big, deep, cello voice.

Onward and upward we went. At that time, it was normal for visitors to climb this path. Unfortunately, landslides and erosion have changed the mountainside drastically and now one can no longer make this climb. Basil and I met many pilgrims on the way, most of them on their way down. They seemed to be running past us as we went slowly upward, but Basil was having none of it. Every single one had to stop. Basil had words for them all, young and old alike. I could tell by the light in their faces, they each went from his presence enriched and touched by God. That was Basil. He was so immersed in God that all he did was give God. I will never forget that day.

Our Lady of Joy

1991–98

Theophane Young, ocso

At a Trappist regional meeting in late 1988, the prior of Hong Kong's Our Lady of Joy Monastery, Dom Benedict Chao, put out an SOS to the entire order for help. The monks were growing older, they had very few new recruits, and the communists were coming. In 1997, the sovereignty of Hong Kong would revert back to the People's Republic of China.

Our Lady of Joy had been established in 1950 when the monastery that had been founded in 1928 in Hebei province in northern China relocated there. During the revolution in China in the 1940s, the Hebei monastery was attacked by communist troops and one of the monks—Father Labre, who was still living in 2006—was shot through the shoulder. By 1947, the community of sixty monks had gone into internal exile in the city of Chengdu in Sichuan province in southwest China. When the communists later arrived in Sichuan, they did not treat the monks well. So Father Vincent, the acting superior, had the monks slip away in twos and threes. Twenty monks arrived in Hong Kong during the late 1940s, exiles from the communist takeover of mainland China. Later, Father Vincent and another monk Father Albert died from the abusive treatment they received in a Chinese jail.

Understandably, the monks in Hong Kong who had originally come from mainland China were not at all comfortable at the prospect of the communist government taking over the British colony of Hong Kong. In 1986, they even created a foundation in

Taiwan with several American Trappists as a fallback community in case they had to leave Hong Kong.

Basil volunteered to go to Our Lady of Joy and was happily accepted by Dom Benedict. There were already two other Americans in the community, one a former Maryknoll missioner in China and Taiwan, and the other a monk from the Trappist community in Vina, California. There was also one Filipino monk there as a volunteer. Another Filipino and another American (myself) were to arrive subsequently.

In the Joy Community, Basil was Dom Benedict's right-hand man: the two conferred together on every issue, and Dom Benedict always took Basil's views very seriously. In the early 1990s, Basil became the novice master for Our Lady of Joy, and later he became the junior master for a number of years. (I had been at the abbey in Spencer, Massachusetts, in 1991 when Basil came back for a visit. He presented a slide show of the Our Lady of Joy Community. Two years later, after a long period of personal and community discernment, I volunteered to go the Hong Kong community.)

Basil was junior master until my Solemn Profession in 1994 and then my advisor and confidant when I was novice master from 1995 to 1998. In these positions, Basil was able to attract a number of new men to the community, including several from Hong Kong and Malaysia who persevered, and others from Canada and Singapore who eventually joined Trappist communities elsewhere.

As a formator (one who helps form new members for religious life), Basil presented the Trappist life as one to be lived seriously, as well as one that should be filled with joy. He enabled the community to pursue a more structured, ongoing formation by helping to set up regular reading and discussion sessions and formation workshops that all the monks in the community were invited to attend. He passed on to us, both in formation sessions and in talks to the community at large, his deep knowledge of the Cistercian Fathers and his broad experience in prayer.

Every two years while he was in Hong Kong, Basil invited someone from outside the community to give a formation workshop, which was also attended by Trappist monks and nuns from around the Asia-Pacific region. So we were treated to lively presentations by Father Chrysogonus Waddell of Gethsemani Abbey in Kentucky, Father Joseph Wong of Big Sur Monastery in California, and Sister Pamela Clinton of Wrentham Abbey in Massachusetts.

There were other practical ways in which Basil made his presence felt at Our Lady of Joy. He successfully urged the resumption of the daily reading of a section of St. Benedict's Rule in the refectory. This had not been done for some years. He convinced the community to brighten up the monastery, which had taken on a dreary appearance. The older monks had been hesitant to spend the money for this if they were going to have to vacate the buildings after 1997. He reintroduced the wearing of the monastic cowl, the long outer garment traditionally worn at the major Offices and Mass, a practice which had been dropped years before due to the high humidity. He used some of the money he received from his Centering Prayer presentations to have a new cowl made for each member of the community, tailored by the monks of his own community, St. Joseph's Abbey in Spencer, Massachusetts. Although it took him awhile, he finally prevailed on the monks to buy and use microphones for the prayers and readings of the Office.

Basil also fostered the reinvigoration of a community spirit at Our Lady of Joy in several ways. First, he chaired the regular community discussions on the various issues that the community faced. Previously, most issues had simply been decided by the elders. For example, the Hong Kong monastery is situated on the eastern side of the island of Lantau, near the Hong Kong Airport that was then being built. (The airport opened in 1998 and Hong Kong Disneyland opened on Lantau in 2005.) A major issue was whether or not to sell the community property and move to a new monastery that would be built by the prospective buyer of the community's land. This was unanimously turned down, especially after Dom Benedict, Basil, and a few other monks of Joy visited the proposed new site and found it unacceptable.

After years of discussion and failed attempts to find alternatives, this remains an issue for the community. How can they use the expanses of monastery land, formerly used for fodder crops and grazing by dairy cows, so the land-scarce Hong Kong government will not be tempted to take it away?

Second, Basil introduced communal, festive, talking meals on the greater feast days of the church year, something which had rarely been done before. Third, he made sure that the younger monks joined the old-timers in working in the small cookie factory the community operated. Now that the elders are in their golden years, the young ones actually run that factory. Fourth, he fostered the expansion of the vegetable and flower gardens that dotted the land near the monastery, so that every monk, including himself, could have a plot to till. Basil loved nature and getting his hands dirty in God's good earth. Indeed, I first met him at Spencer when he was tending a patch of daffodils he had planted.

Basil also gave special attention, in small, loving ways, to the monk in the room next to his, as a monk ought always to do to his elders. This was Father Nicolaus Kao, 109 years old in 2006 and not only the oldest monk in the order, but the oldest Catholic priest in the world. In Basil's time, Father Nicolaus was in his 90s and still tended the flower gardens daily in the Shrine to Our Lady of Fatima that he had built near the Joy guesthouse.

Basil made some unsuccessful efforts to update the Our Lady of Joy community. He strongly suggested that the community convert one of the unused small buildings near the monastery proper into a hermitage that could be used by the monks, as is now done in many other monasteries of the order. But the elders of the community turned this idea down, saying that they were cenobites and had no need of a hermitage. This remains the situation to this day. (Cenobites are monks who stress community life regulated by rules. Hermits live an eremitic life.)

Time and again, Basil introduced the idea into community discussions that Our Lady of Joy should become an abbey (that is, self-governing and autonomous), since it had long since met all the requirements for being so. There was so much opposition to this that it did not happen in Basil's time in Hong Kong. In late 1999, however, the community finally did vote to become an abbey. This was approved by the order, and Dom Anastasius Li, who had been one of Basil's junior monks, is now the second abbot.

Then there was the question of inculturation, or how to adapt the Christian life of the monastery to the local culture. Basil made a small effort in this regard, trying to introduce the use of incense sticks instead of the large metal thurible of incense more common in Western practice. But the community absolutely refused to agree. In many of these attempts to inject new life into the Joy community, I was privileged to be Basil's assistant, so I got to know him on both a personal and social level within our monastic community context, in addition to the official levels dictated by our rule of obedience.

Basil's influence on the wider community around us was considerable. Early on, he took a trip to mainland China, and there visited the sites of the two former Trappist monasteries, now used by the Chinese government for other purposes. He also was able to meet some of the older Trappist monks still living there, all of whom had spent years in prison or under various forms of incarceration for their faith. He often spoke in awesome terms of these courageous men.

The Catholic community of Hong Kong in particular came to know Basil quite well. He regularly held Centering Prayer workshops at the monastery guesthouse and at various locations in the city. He had a regular following of priests, religious, and laity in Hong Kong. They helped him produce three Centering Prayer leaflets, one in English (much used by the non-Chinese and especially by the Filipino Catholics in Hong Kong and in the Philippines); one in classical Chinese script (used by the Chinese Catholics of Hong Kong, with special mention of the prisoners whose chaplains often ask for "refills"); and one in simplified Chinese script (meant for those educated in the new script of mainland China). These leaflets were freely available, together with Basil's many books on the monastic tradition translated into Chinese by monks of Joy for sale at the visitors' entrance to the monastic church. This practice was initiated and maintained by Basil while he lived at Joy. This served as an alternative to the little shop he would have preferred to establish at the monastery guesthouse, had his brother monks seen this as appropriate.

Basil was often sought out as mentor (or as he would put it, "abba," the old Aramaic word for father) and father confessor, especially by the priests of the Hong Kong diocese. With this special ability to help fellow priests, Basil was constantly sought out for his advice. Abba Basil spent many of his waking hours in this role. He also had a special place in his heart for the poor, the homeless, the downtrodden, and the rejected of society.

He employed this sensitivity to the gospel particularly in his sermons during the Sunday Mass when the monastic church was filled with people. He also used this sensitivity in less conspicuous ways with many individuals. Those of us who knew him well were aware of a few of these latter instances, which we knew represented many more known only to God. The fact that Basil was able, despite all of this hands-on service to his fellow humans, to continue producing one spiritual book after another during these years really boggles the mind. The discipline of his monastic training certainly served him well.

Basil tried, bravely and even stubbornly, to learn to speak and read the Mandarin dialect of Chinese, called Putonghua, or "ordinary people's language," which was used in the Office when the monks of Joy chanted their services seven times each day. While he did not succeed, he did learn certain snatches of the language, and so could always be heard belting out the *"Gloria Patri"* in Putonghua at the end of every psalm in the Office.

Finally, especially during these eight years in Hong Kong, Basil found the time and opportunity to travel the world to promote Centering Prayer, making presentations on every continent, plus the Pacific isles and those of the East and West Indies. I know he turned down many more requests than he accepted, but he left behind many thousands of practitioners of contemplative prayer that otherwise would not have know about it. Surely the good Lord and his Mother Mary, for whom Basil had a very deep, vibrant, and personal devotion, understood this interruption of his daily monastic routine in order to provide this service to the Church. This was similar to the pattern established by his famed Cistercian forebear, St. Bernard of Clairvaux, who spent considerable time outside the monastic walls serving the wider Church.

Unfortunately, a number of his brothers were unable to come to the same understanding, and this led to his leaving Our Lady of Joy in mid-1998, just after the public ceremony held to commemorate the seventieth anniversary of the community and the fiftieth anniversary of the arrival of its first monks in Hong Kong. But the Lord brings good out of everything. The subsequent service Basil rendered back in the United States to Cistercian Studies and as Abbot of Conyers, to say nothing of his presence among his beloved brothers of Spencer in his final years, gives witness to this.

From my perspective, Basil was always a monk of Spencer. He had the joy of living and the loving concern for all of his brothers that was the case with all the monks of St. Joseph's Abbey. In my opinion, these qualities go a long way toward understanding why the Spencer community has continued to thrive all these years. This "mark of Spencer" on him, plus his own loving personality, were the substantial gifts he gave to the monks of Our Lady of Joy during his eight years among us.

Basil was a man and a monk of wide experience, but somehow he was able to hang on to a wonderful, childlike approach to the various manifestations of God's will. This was true whether these manifestations elated him, as when he veritably skipped down the cloister (if you can imagine his six-foot, four-inch frame doing so) to tell me of the election of his good friend and mine, Lewis Fiorelli, OSFS, as the superior general of his order, as well as when they hurt him, as when he said with a smile on his face that he had heard that some of his Joy brothers had asked for him to go back to Spencer and that the abbot general had supported their request.

The community of Our Lady of Joy Abbey is growing today. A number of young men are entering, and at least some of that growth can be attributed to Basil's positive influence on its life. The Lord God is good, in himself and in his servants, and for this we are always grateful.

Our Lady of the Holy Spirit

2000–2002

Elias Marechal, OCSO, and Francis Michael Stiteler, OCSO

In the preface to one of Father Basil Pennington's books, Rabbi Lawrence Kushner describes him as "a great, loving bear of a man. His laughter and embrace surround you with nurture. I have never known a man who was more gracefully centered within whom he was, within whom God had made him to be. And this pervades his writing on every level. We have the sense, reading his words, that they come from his innermost essence."

Dom Basil was in many ways a giant of a man. (The titles Dom and Abbot are used interchangeably. Dom is short for the Latin term of address *domne*, lord, given to Benedictine priests in France and England in the Middle Ages.) Even physically, Father Basil looked like someone who stepped out of the Old Testament, with his huge frame and long beard. He was also interiorly a giant in the sense of being one of those rare people who is filled with many, many ideas. Big ideas.

We at Holy Spirit Monastery experienced this for ourselves for the two years Basil was with us. Here was a man who had circled the globe offering ways of connecting with God at a deep level; a monk who had written fifty-seven books and at least a thousand articles; a respected spiritual leader who had facilitated ecumenical and interreligious dialogue—and yet he willingly left it all behind to serve a community of barely fifty monks living on the property of the old Honeycreek Plantation in rural Georgia.

He came here open-hearted after a clear call from the community, and he gave himself to the work as the sixth abbot of the Monastery of Our Lady of the Holy Spirit with all the energy he had. What transpired under his leadership is impressive: an influx of new members, with more waiting in the wings; the construction of a new elevator to enable elderly monks to make their way about a vast four-story building; the establishment of a fruitcake industry that now allows the monks to be more economically self-sufficient; the gradual introduction of new programs into the guest house, rendering it still more of a significant spiritual center for the Southeast; the remodeling of the monastic dining room in a way that expresses more concretely the values of community and fraternal interconnectedness; the initiating of plans for a first-floor infirmary, which would give its inhabitants a deeper sense of connection with the rest of the community and easy access to the main areas of the monastery.

But above all, there was the nurturing spirit of this "great, loving bear of a man" who so encouraged his monks to keep growing in tenderness of heart, in the ways of prayer, in service of one another, in generosity and compassion, in the unique offering of hospitality to guests—whatever their religion or denomination.

When Father Basil offered his resignation as abbot, simply noting—in his characteristically direct and succinct fashion—that he had done all that he could do to help the community, the man's logic was hard to fault. Why stay in a place when—after a manner of speaking—your "mission" has been accomplished?

But Basil was, like Jesus his master, a man of contradictions. He knew and saw himself as a servant of God. He thought of himself as a poor, weak sinner and as someone called and inspired by God. While many people were great devotees of Dom Basil and his writings, others, it must be said, thought that some of what he said and wrote was just a lot of "hot air."

This is typical of those who, like Jesus, are prophets to whom many people are attracted and others are not. We know that Basil was a man of prayer, especially contemplative prayer, and he wanted to share with the whole world that great grace that he had been given. Again, he found a way to do that through his writings. He also did it through the establishment of several different organizations, one of which is the Mastery Foundation, which still exists today.

There are people, even in the church, who don't accept or appreciate the teachings and perspective of Centering Prayer. We think of Dom Basil's friend Mother Angelica, founder of the Eternal Word Television Network. She has often said that she thought Centering Prayer was a waste of time, even though Dom Basil was one of her early supporters, both with his voice and with his financial help. Dom Basil knew how she felt, and he bore that contradiction in friendship. He was quite capable of taking criticism.

Even after he ended his service to us and returned to Spencer in some sorrow, he didn't stop loving us. He didn't stop giving us whatever he could. We have a brand new organ that he sent a year or two after he returned to Spencer. Dom Basil was a great-hearted person whose whole life was given to God. We can look to him to learn about how to be a servant, freely giving oneself to the great mystery of love that God calls us to.

The monks of Conyers will ever remain deeply obliged to Father Basil, not only for his life that he gave to us here but for the life that he gave to the order and to the world. We have little doubt that when he finally died, after having been in a car accident and lingering in intensive care for sixty-seven days, he made that choice himself. The doctors and brother monks took him off the ventilator and explained to him the situation, reminded him of what had already happened, and said that they were willing to try more operations. Dom Basil said, "No. That's enough." He was able to say this with peace, because he knew where he was going. He was on the path to God his entire life. We are sure that it surprised him that the end came in this particular way, but he was ready to go into the arms of his Beloved. Now, may God direct his gifts and talents to whatever place and whatever circumstances call for his assistance.

REFLECTION

Thomas Keating, OCSO

Basil had an enormous capacity for creativity. He would enter a room and all eyes would focus on this enormous presence, overflowing with energy and sympathy and compassion for everyone. He would jump on the bandwagon of any great idea that could bring Cistercian life anywhere around the world. He was there whenever you wanted to get something done. He was a tremendous help to me in the early days of my abbatial experience, and he was truly a spiritual father in the full sense of those words. He really wanted to fill the world with people who had received the message that they also are called to contemplative prayer in the fullness of the Christian life and transformation into Christ. This is what it means to be called to the perfection of holiness that is not a set of particular observances or acts but is a transformation of the heart, mind, and soul into the love of Christ. Basil thought in those terms.

Basil also modeled for us in his death another kind of leadership, the kind of leadership that goes with Christ's passion and death. This is a sublime participation in the sufferings of Christ and of Mary. Being called to the fullness of the transformative process into Christ means you can't win. It means you have to let go of everything you have treasured and loved in your ministry, in your role, in your thoughts, in your talents. Jesus suggests this in that wonderful saying that is often rather weakly translated as, "If you gain your life, you lose it. If you lose it, you will win it." There is another translation that suggests something vastly more profound: "One who seeks to bring his life accomplishments, talents, and self-image to save or preserve that life will bring himself to ruin. But one who brings himself to nothing will find out who he is."

What's left in the tomb when all of our self-identities, our roles, our beloveds, our talents, our thoughts, our feelings, are no longer there? There is just you, your true self, whoever you are. To be able to accept that is to enter into eternal life, trusting the boundless and infinite mercy of God. As far as I can see, there is no other possession in this world worth having except that one. If you have the infinite mercy of God, you don't need anything else.

So Basil emerges now in his servant leadership, that capacity to lead out of powerlessness. This, I suggest, is, or one day will be, the most effective form of leadership—when we have had enough of pride, pretension, power, and especially violence. As Jesus destroyed violence by submitting to it, Basil enters into the fullness of grace that frees our gifts for the fullness of their expression in what we call eternal life.

Part Two

FAMILY MAN

Uncle Bob

Megan Lange

Not long ago, a box showed up on our doorstep. It contained only four items, the entirety of Basil Pennington's worldly possessions. The box contained Basil's Bible, with a thick but worn binding and little things tucked in between the pages. It also had his monastic ring, too large to fit on most anyone's thumb. There was a brass coin that looked as though it had come from a treasure chest and was a memento from his ordination; it had the wear marks of something that had been held and stroked a thousand times. The last item was a hand-painted icon of our beloved uncle's patron, St. Basil the Great.

The box was sent to my husband, Robert, Basil's namesake and grandnephew. Tears filled my husband's eyes as one by one he took the items from the box and inspected them. He gripped the coin, scrutinizing its etched marks and little details. He held it to his forehead and with his eyes closed, he mourned.

Later Robert would say, "When I think of Uncle Bob, I think of a man who knew what it meant to be alive. He spent his life entwined in a web of peacefulness, spirit, and a sense of connectedness. We all strive for that connection with our source, and we all feel a draw toward those who have already found it."

Basil, better known as "Uncle Bob" in our family, made a profound connection with everyone he met. Maybe it was the way he hugged like a giant bear or perhaps the way he instantly became a lifelong friend. He was just that to Jeff, his nephew and my father-in-law, for more than forty years. I would listen to

Jeff recount stories of Uncle Bob at the lake on a wave runner or squeezing into a tiny car with four teenagers.

Jeff said of their friendship, "As Uncle Bob journeyed through life, I was fortunate enough to have been part of his moments. We laughed and shared our experiences. I looked forward to our talks of life, although so different in many ways, on the other hand, so very much alike. He was a light that shone for all who wanted to see. It is sometimes very difficult to put into words all that he was."

The night that Basil's possessions arrived at our house, we had difficulty finding the right words. How can one possibly look at a man's entire anthology of collected items and know what to say. It was only four things. We sat humbled in silence until Robert smiled and said, "He was just always happy."

And he was. Long before I knew Uncle Bob, I'm sure he was smiling and making people smile. My mother-in-law Roree said, "For as long as I can remember, he made the house glow with his presence. His hugs were the most genuine, and he was an amazing listener. He cared and wanted to share with everyone he met a true love of all things and people."

That night, we talked about our wedding and how we used quotes from Basil's writings and how long it had taken us to find just the right ones. Robert told me the story of walking with Uncle Bob in Boston, his first year of college, feeling so detached up until that point, and seeing a man who was willing to make a connection with any person he came across. Basil's Bible sat on the table before us, his name embossed in the upper right hand corner of the dark cover. As I flipped through the pages, I found a single leaf. Perhaps it was from the abbey where he spent his life or a souvenir from one of his travels. The leaf was almost clear but had a hint of green, as though it had just lost its color.

The day Basil died, my sister-in-law April was by his side. There was a small group in the room with him, April and two of his brothers from the abbey. They all sat in his room, eating cookies and telling stories. They took turns holding his hand and just being with him.

"As hard as it was, we tried to make his last hours happy ones," April said. "Then a nurse came in and asked us if we wanted them to freshen him up. We said okay and she asked us to wait down the hall for a moment. After being called back, the nurse informed us that he had just taken his last breath. That was so like my Uncle Bob, to try and spare us from any pain that he could. He knew how much it was going to hurt me to lose him, and he waited until I was out of the room to spare me just a little bit. We circled around his bed and prayed for him. I took his warm hand in my shaky one and held it until his cheeks lost their color. I kissed him good-bye and left."

My husband keeps the brass coin on his easel as he paints. It has the words *christo confixus sum cruci* on the back—"With Christ I am crucified."

My father-in-law, Jeff, said of Basil's passing, "He now resides in the Lord's house, and I'm sure his love of conversation continues to this day. I said good-bye to my dear friend standing in the place where he stood as he blessed the home we now live in. I felt sad, but also overwhelmingly comforted, that although his journey through this life was over, he would forever remain in mine."

Basil Pennington, Uncle Bob, will remain with us all.

Pennington Family History and Myth

M. Basil Pennington, OCSO

It has been some time since I promised to get on tape some of the history and myth of the family that I have often shared with you and other members of the family. This week the Lord has taken to himself Aunt Katy, my father's sister. Last week, Aunt Judy went to join her dear husband, my mother's brother Joe, in the kingdom of heaven.

A generation is almost completely gone now. Uncle Ralph, who is living in Dallas with his daughter Carol, is the only one left, and I understand from Carol that he is experiencing the diminishments of his age.

Possibly I will soon be the senior surviving member of the family. In my generation, there were seventeen cousins. In the following generation, there weren't so many, because there were just three of us brothers. But so far, I think there are twenty-three in the generation after that, or maybe more. And, of course, there are second and third cousins aplenty. It is a joy to watch the generations increase and multiply.

I speak of our family stories as history and myth. Myth is more than story. It is a way in which values, inspirations, and aspirations—something important to family's heritage—is handed down. I suppose as you look at it strictly from the viewpoint of scientific history, you see at times a contradiction between history and myth. But looking at it from a fuller human sense, the mythological has its important role to play in our sense of ourselves as a family, enjoying a heritage.

I see our family emerging out of the mists of Normandy when a knight by the name of Peneul joined the expeditionary force of William the Conqueror. He came from Norman, France, to England and, for his service, was awarded a territory in what is today northwest England and founded what came to be called the village or the town of Pennington—a combination of the Norman name and Anglo-Saxon derivations.

The family eventually built a castle outside of town that has been rebuilt many times. Today, although it is still called Muncaster Castle, it is a large red brick manor house and a high-class bed and breakfast, the present occupants being Pennington's only by marriage and adoption.[1] Of considerable interest to me are the nearby, beautiful ruins of Jervaulx Abbey, which was founded by the Pennington family in the twelfth century—a Cistercian abbey famous for its horses.[2] The seventh abbot was a Pennington, Gamel Pennington. So you see, I am not the first Cistercian abbot in the family.

The next figure who looms large in the family history is Isaac Pennington, who was Lord Mayor of London. In the religiously turbulent era of the sixteenth century, three of Isaac's sons disgraced him by their actions. Young Isaac and William became Quakers and Isaac's stepdaughter married William Penn and came to the United States with those first Pennington's of the Quaker persuasion. Isaac, Jr. was one of the great writers of the Quaker tradition, and his writings are still held in high regard. His wife, Mary, was also a writer. Both of them suffered for their faith and were imprisoned at times. The third son who caused

---

[1] Editor's note: Muncaster Castle is a lively tourist attraction, and their Web site currently includes a page of detail on the history of the Pennington family: http://www.muncaster.co.uk/castle.htm.

[2] Editor's note: Jervaulx Abbey is also a tourist attraction. See http://www.jervaulxabbey.com/.

some disgrace to his father was Alfred, who became a Jesuit priest and was eventually hanged, drawn, and quartered in those dire Elizabethan times.

The family spread and developed in the United States, and it is here where the lines are unclear at times. There is still a certain amount of controversy as to which line of the Pennington family we belong. You can follow the different possibilities in the Pennington family Web site, www.penningtonresearch.org.

This brings us to my Grandpa. He was what they called in those days a "Bible rider." He rode around, Bible in hand, to bring the Good News to the native people in the Midwest. Unfortunately, as he went off riding and preaching, he left his poor wife home with the children, and they suffered a good bit of deprivation. As a result of this, my grandfather, even though he bore the beautiful name of John Wesley Pennington (after the founder of Methodism, John Wesley—a reflection of his own father's great devotion), grew to have little or no regard for organized religion. He was more engaged with the Masons and had more than enough to do to take care of his family.

The story is that when the Cherokee Strip along the Oklahoma and Kansas border opened and runners could stake claims, Grandpa managed to stake a claim, got himself a little schoolhouse, and started teaching. At the end of his first year of teaching, he married the prettiest girl in the class, Olive Kelsey, whose mother was a Cherokee. I dare say there's a good bit of myth there. But he was a teacher and certainly, Grandma was a student. Whether that's the first place they met, I don't know.

Teaching never paid well, and they moved to Colorado in hope of doing better there. Their first son was born there, died very quickly, and was buried there. They eventually moved back to Kansas and got their property outside of Wichita on a small truck farm on Ida Avenue. Their old farmhouse still stands there, high and proud in the middle of the fields now covered with small homes.

To support the growing family, Grandpa got a job as a railway postman, a job he held for several decades. The records, which I found in his desk, showed that he was a very good railway postman. They constantly inspected the accuracy of his work and his speed, and he was always very close to 100 percent.

Of course, holding this job was difficult. It meant that he was away from home a good part of the time. He did the run down from Wichita to Albuquerque, New Mexico, so he would be away three or four days and then would get home for a couple days to work the farm with his boys. He was evidently a fairly strict father, but he had a tender love for his wife. I found in his desk a packet of letters that he had sent home during his first years of marriage. They showed concern, love, and encouragement.

Grandma had Native American features and coloring and found life difficult in Wichita. Sad to say, in those times in Kansas, Native Americans were not treated well. I can remember as a boy watching grandmother braiding her beautiful black hair in the morning. Grandma Pennington was a little woman and her braid went practically down to her ankles. She never cut that hair. She braided it and put it in a big bun. When she went out, although she had little to do with the vanities of this world, she put on a big hat to hide the hair and she powdered her face to lighten her skin so she would not look so much like a Native American. She suffered a good bit from prejudice in her earlier days in Wichita.

The family grew steadily. The oldest daughter, Olive, died when she was four or five and is buried in Wichita cemetery. The oldest surviving son was Dwight, and he was the one who remained with the Quaker tradition. In time, he became the editor of the *Kansas City Star* and built a beautiful home in Kansas City, Missouri, called Pen Oaks.

The next son was Clark. Clark married the girl across the street, Eleanor Anderson, and they had three children. Uncle Clark got a degree in engineering and then joined the army. He had considerable responsibility in the Civil Conservation Corps, which was set up by President Roosevelt during the Great Depression to provide work as well as to develop the natural resources of this country. After the war, he was the military governor of Kyoto in Japan. Eventually he came back and became superintendent at West Point, and I was able to visit him there many times. When Clark retired from West Point, he became a professor in the University of Florida in Gainesville and settled there. He retired to Sarasota and died at the age of ninety-two.

My dad was the third of the surviving sons. He was a very gentle, loving man. His father was a rather strict disciplinarian, and they didn't get along too well from what I hear. So Dad went off at seventeen to join the navy. But his dad did help him get an appointment to Annapolis. Dad did very well at Annapolis but on a summer cruise, between his third and fourth year, he contracted rheumatic fever and his heart was damaged. He was able to complete his year and did very well scholastically, but in his high idealism, he did not accept his commission from the navy nor did he accept the medical discharge or pension that was due him.

By the end of his last year at Annapolis, Dad recovered well enough to travel and decided to visit New York for a couple weeks on his way back to Kansas. One of his classmates arranged for him to stay with his family, and it was in the course of those couple of weeks that he met my mother. When it came time to leave, he asked her if there was any chance of her marrying him. When she said yes, he decided to stay in New York. He'd been very impressed during his navy days by the faith and devotion of some of the Catholic sailors he got to know. Now, getting to know my mother, he began to take the Catholic Church seriously. He studied the Catholic faith and was received into the church before they were married on November 11, 1928. He eventually went back to Kansas six years later with his wife and two children.

Let's go on through his brothers and sisters. Next came three sisters. First of all was Lenore. Mother told me how nervous she was when she went out there to Kansas to meet Dad's family. And the sisters told me how nervous they were when they heard that this girl from New York was coming. But they related so well that when Lenore was ready to step out on her own, she came to New York and lived with us for a while. Inspired maybe by my father, she studied the Catholic faith for a while and was engaged to a Catholic man. It didn't work out, and she went on to find a career with Christian services. She did mission work with the migrant workers and the field workers down in the South. She became an executive in the YWCA, living a very dedicated life. When she was fifty, her sweetheart from her high school days became a widower and came courting. They got married and had a dozen or so years of happy married life. They retired to the woods of northern Minnesota. It was only after her husband's death that she moved to Florida to be near her brother Clark.

The next girl was Lois. Lois also came to live with us in New York after she left home. She met a dashing young man by the name of Frenchy Farone. The Farone family was quite a family, to say the least. Mama Farone had twenty-five children, and they pretty much ran the town of Saratoga, New York, which was, of course, built around the horse racing track up there. The summer I was twelve, I went to Saratoga and stayed for seven weeks with Aunt Lois and Uncle Frenchy. At that time, they had two girls.

Later, two boys came along. It was an interesting experience. We had been, since Dad's death, quite poor. Even before that, in the Depression era, things were lean, and it seemed I was always hungry. When I was in Saratoga, there was plenty to eat—good Italian food in great abundance. I think I put on thirty-five pounds that summer. I had to buy new trousers to come home. It was wonderful.

Eventually, Frenchy had to leave Saratoga and they went out to Arizona. Then, sad to say, he left Lois and went to Mexico and married someone there. But when he came down with cancer, Lois went and brought him home and nursed him. So, at the end, he died in peace and received a good Catholic funeral in Arizona. Lois herself never joined the Catholic Church, although she looked at it at times and took care to raise her children as good Catholics. She bought a grave for herself next to the graves of Grandma and Grandpa and Lenore and Katy in Wichita and on a July day not long ago, she was buried there. Lois's children gave her lots of grandchildren and great-grandchildren.

Katy went to Friends University and then on to medical school. She finished her training just at the time of the Second World War, when so many of the male doctors were going off to the army. So she immediately had quite a practice. Katy was a very little woman, like her mother. She was so little that they had to place a milk box next to the operating table so that she could stand on top of it. It was because she had such delicate little fingers that she was able to do these operations on children's hearts before they had microscopic surgery.

Katy became one of the top surgeons for children's heart operations. With her friend Sister MaryAnn, she helped develop St. Joseph's Medical Center in Wichita. Children were flown in from all over the United States so that she could operate on them. Katy brought an awful lot to her ministry of healing. She became known and loved throughout Wichita. Whenever I held a workshop or celebrated a Mass in Wichita, I always had people come and say. "Your aunt took care of me," "Your aunt took care of my children," or "Your aunt took care of my family or my parents."

Next in line was Uncle John, John Wesley Pennington, Jr. We didn't have much contact with Uncle John. He became an engineer and eventually became head of the Caterpillar Corporation. But he had a real sense of family, and when Mom needed somebody, he was there for her. My mother could always call him if she needed help.

The next in line was Neal. He went off to the naval air corps, studied at Pensacola, and got his wings. He served in the Pacific. In February 1942, his plane went down in the Pacific. At the time, he was engaged to be married to a fine Catholic girl and was preparing himself to become a Catholic.

The youngest of the family was Uncle Ralph. Ralph got an appointment and went through West Point during wartime, when it was reduced to a three-year course. It was during that time that I got to know Ralph better, although I knew him some from my boyhood visits to Wichita. At West Point, he met Ann, a nurse from North Carolina, and they were married soon after his commissioning. Of his first twenty years as an officer, I'm told he spent eighteen years studying and getting more degrees and developing strategic programs for the army. He is something of a mathematical genius. When he was getting ready to take his retirement at the end of twenty years, his father told him he couldn't do that, because it wouldn't be fair to the taxpayers who had put so much into him. At the same time, the army offered to build him the biggest computer in the world if he'd stay on board. And he did, for a few more years.

Mom and Dad were married on November 11, 1928, and my oldest brother was born on September 28, 1929. I was born in 1931. Tom was born five years later in 1936. Dad and Mom certainly wanted more children, but Mother had health problems after my birth and then Dad died in 1938. The rheumatic fever, which caused him to leave the navy, reoccurred in 1938, and struck his heart. They didn't yet have the serum, which they developed five years later. So there was nothing that could be done for him. For twenty weeks, we watched him fade away.

Grandma Pennington came from Wichita, and I can remember her sitting by his bed, night and day. That September, we had a tremendous hurricane that ripped through Long Island, where we were living, and left us without electricity. Indeed, a large tree destroyed part of our house. I remember Grandma sitting there in the candlelight, watching my dad as he slowly faded. He died on December 7, 1938.

He had gotten a job at the telephone company, and the telephone company was very loyal to its employees. He therefore was able to work all through the Depression, and after he died they continued his salary for a year, which helped Mother get through the first, difficult period. They had built a beautiful home in Freeport, Maine, in 1936–37, but Mother had to put the house up for rent and move back to Brooklyn to live with her mother, Grandma Kenny.

Mother, who never wanted to work and never prepared for a career, found great difficulty getting a job. When she finally did get a job working at an office in a hospital, it paid something like ten cents an hour. They were very lean, difficult times. She helped support her mother and take care of the three of us as well as herself. It was only some years later when Marian was studying law, that we found out that Mom should have received a pension for Dad's service in the navy and his medical disability.

By that time, the war had come and Mother was able to get a much better job. We went to Our Lady of Angels School. My older brother, Dale, went to Brooklyn Tech after grade school, which was sort of a special public school for those who qualified. He was on the swim team there and was quite a swimmer. As soon as he was old enough, he got jobs as a lifeguard.

The first summer after Dad died we spent with Uncle Clark on Lake Ontario. The second summer, we went to Camp Dunnigan, a camp run by the Knights of Columbus to which Dad had belonged. I became a junior Knight of Columbus. It was a very primitive camp, and Uncle Clark didn't think it was a very good place. So the next summer we went to Camp St. Agnes, a parish camp belonging to one of the churches in New York. It was a very fine camp, and we had a good summer there. We went back again the next summer. The year after that, we tried another camp—a Salesian camp in Goshen. It was interesting— the trotting races were in town. Unfortunately, Dale had an accident there while horseback riding and broke his arm. The Salesians thought they could get me to join their order, so we kept in touch through the years.

Grandma Kenny died in October 1944, and soon after we sold the house in Brooklyn and moved back to Freeport. Mother was able to get a job there in the hospital, and she continued after Dale went off to Korea and I went off to the monastery. She lived there with Tom, who went through Chamanade and Fordham, and then after his marriage moved out to the Midwest to continue his education there.

My mother was blessed with a happy and peaceful life in those last years and the joy of her grandchildren and my brother Dale. She went off to heaven in 1980. I once had a theology teacher who maintained that death ultimately was a willed act. Many people will to leave because their body is no longer a habitable place. There are those who will it because they felt their life was complete, and some who will it for other reasons. I'm told my Grandfather Kenny was very opposed to Aunt Marian marrying Uncle Skip. On the day of the wedding, as they were about ready to leave for the church, he just sat down in a chair and died. He said he'd rather die than see her marry him. The wedding was put off for a couple weeks, but then they did get married.

I always thought Mother had prepared for her death. I had seen her in the hospital a couple years before when she was in intensive care and she said to me with great simplicity, "If God wants to take me to be with your father, I'm ready. If he wants to leave me to take care of your brother, I'm ready to stay." The next year, Dale got married again, and I guess mother felt that her work was complete.

The family was going to get together on August 12 and 13 before I left for India. So everyone made arrangements to gather on Long Island. On August 10, Mom was at Dale's house. He always wanted her to come and live there, but she always said she should have her own place. She wanted to leave her family completely free, although she always loved to be there. But that night, she asked if she could stay. Yes, of course, she was most welcome. She could use Mickey's room. She went upstairs at about 8:00 PM or so and lay down. When Mickey came into her room later, she found Grandma had gone off to heaven.

As I was driving down from Spencer the next day, I was wondering about something. When a priest is ordained, after his hands are anointed with oil, they are wrapped in a cloth— it's called a maniturge. Mary Jane had embroidered a beautiful one for me with my motto, "For me to live is Christ." After the anointing and the presentation of the chalice and paten, the priest's hands are wiped on this cloth. Then it is rolled up and given to the priest's mother. The tradition is that it is to be placed in the mother's hands in her coffin so everyone will know she is the mother of a priest. I wondered if I would be able to locate my maniturge to put in Mother's hands.

When I got to her apartment, I found it, already out on the table, in its little box, waiting for me. Also, on the table were eight envelopes, one for each of her grandchildren. But everything else was gone. All her clothes were gone. She'd cleaned out her drawers and given away everything. She always said she didn't want to be any trouble to others when she went.

There's one more thing that should have been a sign to us. I remember when her mother died, she was laid out in a beautiful blue dress with a lovely lace collar. As I stood by the coffin with Mom, she said, "Oh how I wish I had gotten that dress for your Grandmother while she was alive, so that she could have enjoyed it." The spring before Mom went home to heaven, she bought a dress just like that and she wore it at First Communions and weddings that spring and really enjoyed it. There it was for her to be buried in. Her life was complete. She was ready to go to be with my father in heaven. I hope every one of us will be able to lead our lives in such a way that we feel complete and have done all that we want to do and that we're ready to go home to heaven.

I expect to spend the rest of my life quietly here at Spencer, having spent about forty years traveling all over the world sharing Christian meditation and having served as superior at the monastery in Ava and as abbot at Our Lady of Holy Spirit Abbey. I think my life's work, in good part, is complete. So I look forward to some quiet years of contemplation and prayer. I hold every member of my family in my heart's prayer, and I hope in that way to be a blessing to each one.

The Penningtons and Their Religious Vocations through the Centuries

Jasper Pennington

Numerous Penningtons have shared an interest in the interior life and in the religious vocation. This is a brief accounting of a few of them.

The life and writings of Isaac Pennington, Jr. (1617–79), the seventeenth-century Quaker divine, illustrate as well as any the interest in spirituality and in religious vocation that seems to have long roots and continual interest by members of the Pennington family. Isaac, the Quaker, comes midway in our family history, long after the appointment of Robert Pennington as Abbot of Waltham Cross Abbey in Essex in 1168 and before the appointment by Pope Lucius III of Jocelinus de Pennington in 1181 as eighth abbot of Furness and long before the writings of M. Basil Pennington, Chester Pennington, Edgar Legare Pennington, Levi Talbot Pennington, and others.

The religious turbulence of the sixteenth and seventeenth centuries in England made a Puritan of Sir Isaac Pennington (1587–1661). He was Lord Mayor of London, friend and neighbor of John Milton, and sheriff of the Tower of London, sending Archbishop Laud to the scaffold on January 10, 1645. He sat in on the trial of Charles the First (although not signing the death document) and died in the Tower on the restoration of the monarchy and the return of Charles the Second.

This time was remarkable for its religious activity and fervor. John Foxe and the Quakers seemed to rise up out of the soil during the sixteenth and seventeenth centuries. The need for a legitimate heir had driven Henry VIII to reject the papacy and loot the valuable and nontaxable properties of the Church. Many families observed the rites of the newly established church of Henry VIII and others kept to the ways of the old (Roman Catholic) church under threat of fines and imprisonment as the Tudors and following monarchs waffled back and forth over the papacy and religious toleration.

This turbulence, with its desire for religious certainty, led Isaac, Jr., to become a Quaker, a prolific writer of tracts and one of the first men of wealth to join the Quaker movement, along with his wife, Mary Pennington Proude Springett, widow of Sir William Springett. Mary's daughter Guliema Maria Posthuma Springett was the first wife of William Penn and her stepbrothers Edward and John Pennington came to Philadelphia, where they continued the tract warfare of the age.

During this time, in the 1620s, Arthur, another son of Isaac the Puritan, became a Roman Catholic priest at a time of great danger and was probably ordained on the Continent. The fact that he believed intensely in his calling in spite of the legal restrictions leads me to refer to him as Arthur the Recusant. His father probably disowned him along with his brother Isaac the Quaker.

In a time not noted for religious tolerance, Arthur's brother Isaac the Quaker wrote to a friend: "I should be glad, if the Lord saw good, that I might see my Brother before I die; and if I did see him, I should not be quarrelling with him about his religion, but embrace him in brotherly love, and in the fear of the Lord."

The reform movements of the medieval church shook up all who called themselves Christians and led to divisions, separations, religious sects, new communities, political reactions, economic challenges, and religious intolerance. Throughout this period, these three Pennington's struggled to find their places as Puritan, Quaker, and Roman Catholic.

In this same period, the Reverend Alan Pennington (1670–1728) became Preacher General of the Dominicans after attending the English College in Rome.

The Reverend Dom Edmund Pennington (1757–94) of Lancashire, was caught up in the tribulations of the Sisters of the Monastery of Our Lady of Good Hope in Paris. The French Revolution began in July 1789 and the status of Catholic monastics, secular clergy, cathedral clergy, and the visible signs of the Church itself were in danger and disorder. Dom Pennington helped the nuns in their ejection from France in 1795 and finally aided their escape to England, where it was now legal for Mass to be celebrated as long as they lived quietly.

A man who encouraged thoughtful discussion and writing was the Reverend Montague Pennington (1762–1849), an Anglican priest who supported a group of upper-class women in London to discuss and write about the political, literary, and religious issues of the day. The Reverend William Pennington-Bickford, Rector of St. Clement Danes, London from 1910–41, helped the parish and city in the recovery of London after World War I. His interest in hymnology produced two sets of hymnbooks for use in the parish. He also helped restore St. Clement's, a Christopher Wren building.

The interests of the Penningtons in religion and in a religious vocation was also prevalent in the American Colonies and later in the new United States. *Talento ad missiones et opera pia* (all his qualities of a high order) was the conclusion of Thomas Hughes about the Reverend Francis Pennington, SJ (1644–99) of Worcestershire. He and his brother the Reverend John Pennington, SJ (1647–85) sailed to Maryland with the Royal

Fleet in 1675, where Francis succeeded the Reverend Michael Forster as superior of the Maryland Mission.

The Reverend Dennis Pennington helped found Methodism in Kentucky when he and his brother Walter accompanied Henry Clay from Virginia to the Louisville area. He and his brother traveled from Virginia to Kentucky via the "ride and tie" method used when two people have one horse. One person rides beyond the second traveler and ties up the horse and goes on by foot. The second traveler does the same and so both get to ride halfway to their destination and the horse is kept rested. Dennis was also an architect and designed the first statehouse for the Indiana Territory that can still be seen at Corydon, Indiana, just across the river from Louisville.

The Reverend Levi Talbot Pennington (1879–1978) had an impressive life of ministry to others as a journalist, teacher, pastor, and academic. He was born in Michigan of Quaker parents, his father being a one-time pastor of the Quaker Church in Ypsilanti Township, Washtenaw County, Michigan. During World War I, he became a friend of Herbert Hoover and helped found the American Friends Service Committee that saved thousands of lives from starvation in France, Germany, Britain, Russia, and Belgium. In later life he became president of George Fox University in Newberg, Oregon, and wrote several books of poetry and reminiscences.

The Brotherhood of St. Barnabas in Gibsonia, Pennsylvania, was part of the Anglo-Catholic Movement of the early nineteenth century. Although not a monastic community in the usual sense, the Brotherhood was dedicated to the care of the poor and those men and boys who were terminally ill. Brother Charles H.L. Pennington (1895–1965) was a young engineer from the University of Toronto when he first visited Gouverneur Provoost Hance, the founding father of the Brotherhood in 1900.

Tuberculosis was the most dreaded killer in the opening decades of the twentieth century and those without financial support died uncared for in rooming houses and in the streets. Some of these unfortunates were admitted to St. Barnabas Home, where they were cared for throughout their illnesses and prayed for in their deaths. The work of Brother Hance and Brother Pennington and others of their Brotherhood is carried on today as the St. Barnabas Health System in Gibsonia, Pennsylvania.

The Reverend Edgar Legare Pennington (1891–1951) was born in Madison, Georgia, and received his doctor of sacred theology in 1937 from the University of the South in Sewanee, Tennessee. Edgar had been one of the survivors of the sinking of the USS *Abraham Lincoln* by a German submarine off the coast of Spain in 1918. Twenty-six men perished and Edgar was one of those rescued after eighteen hours on rafts and lifeboats. He served as a parish priest until 1943, when he became a navy chaplain serving in the Pacific. He returned to the United States as rector of St. John's Church, Mobile, Alabama, and continued his research and teaching career. Dr. Pennington was a specialist in the history of the Anglican Church in the American Colonial Period. He was an excellent teacher, tutor to seminary students, examining chaplain in Georgia, Alabama, and Florida and a man beloved by those who met him.

The Reverend Leslie Talbot Pennington (1899–1974) was a Quaker born in Spiceland, Indiana, whose ministry led him to be pastor of First Parish in Cambridge, Massachusetts, from 1935–44. He felt that every personal problem was a social problem and every social problem was a personal problem and saw himself as a servant of God in approaching these and other issues. The Reverend Chester Arthur Pennington (1916–2005) was for over twenty years pastor of Hennepin United Methodist Church in Minneapolis, Minnesota, one of the great

Methodist congregations in the United States. A graduate of Drew University, he was a prolific writer on spiritual issues facing contemporary society.

Over the years, Basil and I talked about this family background and we shared some of the information from my ongoing research, giving me bits and pieces of information for further research. Basil was at my ordination at the Church of the Ascension, Rochester, New York, in May 1974, presenting me a red stole from the Holy Rood Guild at Spencer Abbey.

From 1973 until 1981 when St. Bernard's Seminary in Rochester, New York, was closed, I gathered and established the Fulton John Sheen Archives that are now part of the Diocesan Archives. Archbishop Sheen was quite unlike Basil except in his interest in the life of prayer and its transforming power. Sheen often got me mixed up with Basil, probably because neither of our names are common. Both Basil and Sheen lived very public lives deeply empowered by their spiritual grounding, a grounding which made possible their public ministries.

Basil often visited our house in Ypsilanti, Michigan, where I was rector of the historic St. Luke's Episcopal Church for eighteen years. He usually came with jams and jellies that we all enjoyed. He was such a giant of a man that we were surprised when he seemed intimidated by our dog, Dilly, only saying, "What big teeth you have, Dilly!" as she stood patiently waiting for some petting. Generally after a visit, I drove him on to Kalamazoo for the Cistercian Studies Conference, a component of the annual international Congress on Medieval Studies at Western Michigan University, a wonderful part of his legacy as a scholar.

In writing this brief article about some of those in the Pennington family who have pursued their interests in the interior life and in religious vocations with fortitude, integrity, and faith, I have tried to show something of their different approaches to God as the center of one's being without this turning into a major thesis. There are many more Pennington clergy not mentioned here.

REFLECTION

Cynthia Pennington

Faith is a small word with a large meaning. To me it has always signified complete trust, a belief in something without physically seeing or touching it.

I met Uncle Bob (my husband's uncle) when I was in my early twenties. Over the next two decades, we often discussed faith. I willingly and openly listened to his experiences, trying to glean some insight into God, something he knew that I did not. When he passed away, and I drove to Spencer to see him for the last time, I thought about our conversations and how much I would miss them.

Kneeling before Uncle Bob's casket, crying as I looked at his peaceful face, I wanted to ask him if it was all worth it. Was heaven and being in God's presence all we had imagined it would be? On my way home, I thought about how his presence filled a room, how his voice was so comforting. How I loved the fact that Uncle Bob had married Neil and me, had baptized all my children, and how happy I had been to be at his side to celebrate the fiftieth anniversary of his commitment to God. It was then that it hit me, and I knew. Yes, it had all been worth it, and I was certain that heaven and being in God's presence was so much more than we had ever imagined.

All those years of searching Uncle Bob's words for answers, when all the answers were sitting right in front of me, with a white beard and twinkling blue eyes. It was written all over him. The peace that walked into the room when he did, the happiness that always shone in his eyes, the security he felt in the path he had chosen. Uncle Bob was the embodiment of faith in God and all it could bring you. It dawned on me that I had never fully given control of my life to God. I still held on to the notion that I could somehow "steer my own ship." I had the meaning of faith securely in my head but its wonders had eluded my heart and soul.

I vowed on that day to think of Uncle Bob every time I felt the pride of being in control, every time I was tempted to listen to my inner voice instead of asking God what he wanted me to do. Since then, I have given my life back to the Lord. I have studied the Bible and searched for God's hand in my world, and much to my joy, I have discovered that he is all around me. When I see Uncle Bob again—and I will—I am going to thank him for bringing me home, for helping me feel it is all worth it, for helping me find peace. Basil Pennington was a great man, not because of his stature, not because of his travels, not because of anything he accomplished. He was a great man because of his faith, and I was honored to know him. I love you and miss you, Uncle Bob.

Part Three

MAN OF PRAYER

Reflections on Monastic Meanings in the Twenty-first Century

Laurence Freeman, OSB

The following reflections are offered in gratitude to honor the memory of Father Basil Pennington, to whom this volume is dedicated. He was one of a small band of monks since the Second Vatican Council in the early 1960s—the beginning of the "World Church" as Karl Rahner called it—who made significant and lasting contributions to the spiritual life and consciousness of his contemporaries.

Speaking from an ancient tradition and from training in time-honored ways of formation, he and monks like Thomas Merton, Bede Griffiths, and John Main understood the spiritual crisis of the secular world better than many beyond the cloister. Fired by an intense zeal and energy, they sacrificed their stability in order to travel, and their silence in order to speak or write in service of a world that had largely lost its ability even to understand what monks or monasteries mean. They were not seeking vocations for their houses or necessarily speaking about monasticism at all. Yet they were very much monks.

What they had to share with the world rose from a pure and direct source in their monastic life. Their effect upon the spirituality of the modern world is easily seen, and its variety reflects their very different gifts, personalities, and callings. Although they reflected some glory on the institutions that bred and freed them for their apostolates, some people would say that they weakened or abandoned their monastic calling to turn as much as they did toward the needs of the world. Surely, critics would say, the true monk witnesses by being invisible, stable, and silent, not by traveling and teaching beyond the cloister as much as they (or St. Bernard or St. Romuald) did. Did not these monks, for monks they remained, in fact also serve their contemporary and future monastic brethren by the very challenge their contemplative witness presents and through the light they shed on the tradition that formed them?

To attempt to trace the thread of the monastic meaning they illuminate, it is necessary to place these great monk-teachers and their monasticism in a contemporary social and historical context.

First, what drew them out of the cloister? Thomas Merton's own monastic journey from *Seven Storey Mountain* to *Contemplation in a World of Action* illustrates the length of the journey he made. He entered the monastery at a time when the relationship between monastic life and the outer world was clearly defined by varying degrees of exclusion of the world. Permission to leave the monastery was rarely given. The world in the form of guests was welcome to visit and bathe in the monastic atmosphere, but the Benedictine and especially the Trappist monk was not expected to go far in the opposite direction.

In an important sense, this is the norm. If all monks were to engage with the world as much as Merton and Pennington and others did, the monastery would risk becoming a religious hostel for people with external apostolates, a place to come and recharge. Yet exceptions prove the rule. And the exceptional lives of these modern missionary and contemplative monks challenge the very significance and purpose of the life that defined them, but which they also redefined.

The world changed very rapidly in their lifetimes. Eventually the Church responded to this change with its own prophetic *aggiornamento,* turning from its Augustinian self as a "perfect society" in a siege mentality with the world to respect, to serve and engage with the world and even with other faiths. The world had moved rapidly from an agrarian or industrial mentality toward an intense technological, information-based network, and from local non-self-communicating entities to a rapidly globalizing consciousness. In the process, faith lost its meaning for many, and they found that they had no time for it. The old forms of belief and devotional habits fell into disuse as the pressures of modern life increased. Faith faltered as the "perfect society" showed its wounds, church attendance crashed, and predictions were made of the end of religion in the age of science. But at the same time, a whole dimension of faith and religion that had languished in the shadows and on the margins of the Church emerged into the light and regained its true centrality.

The restoration of the contemplative dimension of Christian faith resulted from the Second Vatican Council's radical theological reorientation as well as the impact of Eastern spiritualities upon Western society. These two causes were often confused. Christian teachers who taught contemplation were accused of importing "Eastern" ideas and practices and thus diluting their faith. As the heady optimism of the Council Fathers gave way to pastoral realities, the speed of reform changed and gears crashed as some attempts were made to go into reverse. Thanks in great measure to the courage and sense of mission of the new contemplative teachers who (as is said of poets) created the taste by which they were enjoyed, ignorance of the Christian contemplative tradition diminished and the true meaning of interreligious dialogue increased.

These new contemplative teachers were not all monks or religious, but their pioneers frequently came from these traditions in the Church—a sign of the impact of monasticism and its varied descendants on other forms of religious life. This meaning is to be a prophetic, even if misunderstood, witness to the direction in which the Spirit is moving the people of God. Monks, as Bede Griffiths liked to point out, are the inheritors of the biblical prophetic groups, and so in a particular sense the "prophetic order" of the Church.

Increasingly, "spiritual" rather than "religious" became the preferred way in which Westerners liked to understand this side of themselves. Although a corresponding rise of Pentecostal Christianity and some over-publicized fundamentalism accompanied it, a contemplative spirituality began to grow and sank deep roots into the mind and lifestyle of the Church. General exceptions to this were seminaries and novitiates that made minor or confused changes, usually in a pastoral or psychological direction to the conventional formation of the upcoming generation of Church leaders and teachers.

At the same time, a newly enfranchised laity, though still largely excluded from organizational responsibility in the Church, began to grow in contemplative experience. From this maturity they began to teach contemplation, as can be seen in the contemplative networks of Contemplative Outreach and the World Community for Christian Meditation, both founded by monks. The monks, who were a link with the contemplative sources for this new ministry among the laity, not only collaborated but encouraged this development. It was a reminder to many ordained monks that their way of life was originally a lay movement. Monks of the desert had fled from ordination. St. Benedict, whose Rule shaped Western monasticism, was not himself a priest and had reservations about allowing priests into the monastery at all.

The "analogical predicate" of Thomas Aquinas, which postulates that what we say of God is not literal, nor is it only metaphorical, began to make sense experientially to those who had never heard of it. Contemplative experience sharpens the mind and gradually develops consciousness from the mythical toward the postrational stage. Scripture was discovered by many Catholics to be a new source of spiritual wisdom and growth when read with deeper attention than they could usually give to it in the Sunday readings at Mass.

Lectio returned with new energy to the Christian life. While the breakdown of a social moral consensus magnified the confusion of the moral maze, the search for inner authority compensated for an excessive reliance on external authority. People listened to the voice of conscience with less fear of being condemned. As the apophatic aspect of theology and spirituality re-asserted its place as a complement to the cataphatic realms of dogmatic theology, many looked to monasteries as places to find friendlier and deeper sapiential teaching. Significantly, this did not lead to a great increase in monastic vocations or even to a particularly strong revival of contemplative practice in Christian monasteries. But at the same time, Buddhist monasteries and *sanghas* were developing strongly with a single-minded focus on contemplative discipline.

Nevertheless, for most Christians interested in contemplative prayer, the atmospheric association of contemplation and monasticism was too engrained to break. As monasteries became more hospitable, this relationship strengthened. So, while monks declined numerically, monastic communities became increasingly popular places to withdraw to go on retreat in order to strengthen the lay person's contemplative qualities of silence, solitude, and stillness. However, the teachings needed to maintain the contemplative life in the world were seldom offered from the monastery itself, with the exceptions, at the time, of some of the monasteries of the pioneering monks I have mentioned, such as Basil at Spencer, John Main at Montreal, and Bede Griffiths at Shantivanam.

Today, as many monasteries face closure for lack of numbers and often lack the will or "good zeal" necessary to survive, the contemplative renewal of the Church continues to accelerate with increasing support from bishops and clergy. It is happening in all the churches of Christianity as it becomes more obviously seen as the foundation of ecumenical unity, especially that "spiritual ecumenism" encouraged today by Cardinal Walter Kasper and Rowan Williams, the Anglican Archbishop of Canterbury.

So, in a world like ours where contemplation is no longer felt to be restricted to the monastic life, what is a monk today? Perhaps what he or she has always been, according to the desert father who was first asked this question 1,600 years ago: "A monk is one who asks himself every day, 'What is a monk?'"

As the contemporary context of contemplative renewal suggests, what looks like a monk is only a visible expression of an archetype active in every human being. In the monk we see a sign of that single-minded search for God that St. Benedict identifies as the basis for admitting a candidate to monastic training. "Does he truly seek God?" The ancient monks knew that, although this must define the monk, it could hardly be less than equally applicable to everyone else. More or less consciously, we all seek God as an absolute or at least have the instinct and capacity to do so. The monk shows this just as a married man and woman express the universal human need for love, union, and family. Even Jesus in his historically and culturally conditioned humanity could not express every archetype at work in the process of human wholeness.

Thus there are specialized—but always complementary— vocations. Monks and priests are rarely seen any more as closer to God than married couples or those living single in the world. This has contributed to a certain crisis of identity in the monastic life. Why become a monk then? Is the monastery the best place to seek God? Many monastic candidates leave after asking this question during the period of their novitiate or simple vows. Nevertheless, as monasticism is as ancient an archetypal expression as civilization itself and seems to acquire greater importance as civilization is threatened or in decline, it is unlikely that all monasteries will die out or that monks will be reduced to museum exhibits.

The monastic archetype is inbuilt. Yet like all archetypes it takes shape in a context. As a recent Benedictine Abbot Primate, with an unparalleled firsthand knowledge of existing monasteries, said recently in response to the question of what he thought of the future of monasteries: "The survival of the fittest—those who adapt will survive, the rest will become extinct."

Monasteries there will always be, if fewer and smaller. We imagine monasticism in terms of the great medieval institutions but forget that the majority of monasteries in history were small local priories. If for no other reason, there will always be monasteries because some people can only survive in a monastery. There will always be some kind of monastic life to provide a loving, safe home and refuge for the "fools of God," some with advanced degrees, whom the world despises or who cannot cope with the world.

But will there also be a kind of monastic life that witnesses to the rest of the world with spiritual authority and power, compassion and utility? If so, how might it emerge from the critical and often paralyzed state of Western monasticism today? There is no doubt that monasteries are interesting to modern Westerners, as in recent and popular television shows and films, and in dozens of books published every year. But is it a monasticism that deeply resonates with the spiritual search and contemplative life that more people than ever are trying to live in the world? Is the interest in monasticism only a faintly nostalgic memory of a hidden archetype at work or is it an interest in a mystical teaching and spiritual engagement with the needs and problems of people in the world?

There is evidence that monasticism can still rise to this higher challenge. Some ancient monastic congregations have renewed themselves in the spirit of the times and, while remaining small in numbers, exert a wide-ranging influence on the spiritual life of their immediate neighbors. New forms of monastic life are also developing, in Europe especially, like the French Jerusalem Community or the Bethlehem Community. These movements are new branches of the old tree, often encouraged by existing conventional monasteries with whom they maintain friendly relations.

But their tone and way of interaction with the world is different from their monastic forebears. While often "traditional" in appearance, they are free to think freshly. Freer than older communities to be creative and to synthesize traditions, they often bring together symbols, spiritual wisdom, and liturgical practices from both Eastern and Western Christianity. They have confident identities of their own, but they also adapt to the needs and timetables of working people in ways that older monasteries could find traumatic. These new forms of monastic life attract the young people who are looking for community not as a safe refuge from the world or to seek false certainties but in order to sustain an ever-deepening and transformative life of prayer—a goal that they often found older monasteries were unable or unwilling to support at the level they needed.

Monasticism continues to feed the heart of the Church, but its capacity to do so derives from an institutionally marginal position. Its influence is always disproportionate to its numbers. Its new forms, such as the so-called lay monasticism of the oblate tradition, emerge under the influence of the Spirit through the lives of individuals and small communities. The Rule of St. Benedict says that there are different kinds of monks, but it shows little interest in the differences except to point out the shortcomings of those who live outside the community and who are enslaved to their own wills and appetites. The strong monk for Benedict is the one who lives in community under an abbot preparing for single-handed combat in the desert at some future time.

Fundamentally the monk, even in community, is *monachos*: a single one. There is a paradox here, even a contradiction, whose roots lie in the experience of prayer itself. Renunciation of self leads to the discovery in joy of the true self. Solitude, as Merton said, opens to selfhood in God. Contemplation, as Main said, leads to community. Whatever else the monastery may be and whatever its apostolate, it can hardly be a monastery if it is not a place of prayer. What does prayer mean today? Can the monastery answer this to the satisfaction of the spiritual hunger of the world? The monk is a person of prayer. Prayer is the monk's business. His or her greatest gift is the gift of prayer. And prayer is the greatest hunger and need of our time. The future of monasticism is being shaped by how it relates to this need.

> We do not pray in order to get benefits from God but to become like God. Praying itself is good. It calms the minds, reduces sin, and promotes good deeds.
> (Origen, *On Prayer*)

What Origen wrote in the third century speaks sharply and clearly to people today who are seeking spirituality rather than religious authority. Even if this dichotomy is a false one, it is a popular perception. The sense of prayer as a social obligation, the fee paid to belong to a religious institution or the idea that it is a way of manipulating the will of God in our direction are both redundant. To the first Christians *lex orandi est lex credendi*, the way you live is the way you pray, prayer authenticates or exposes one's entire value system.

For many people today, prayer, increasingly and in particular, means contemplation. This is what it also meant to Jesus. His teaching on prayer—interiority, trust, brevity of words, freedom from anxiety, mindfulness, and living in the present moment as the Sermon on the Mount makes clear—show him to be a teacher of contemplation. To the first monks, prayer meant essentially that "prayer of fire," which is contemplation leading on to mystical union with God in the prayer of Christ. For Benedict, the monastery is a place where one prepares for this through the elementary disciplines of controlling one's own wayward will and harmonizing the inner life through outward disciplines. Today perhaps the monastery has also to be more than this. It is called to become the "living centre of contemplation" that Bede Griffiths said every monastery has to be.

The Rule does not speak much about prayer in the form of the Divine Office. It emphasizes the mindful harmony of voice and heart that should be sustained in the psalmody. Otherwise, there are few references to the effects of having private prayer extended by the Holy Spirit and of praying in the heart during the day. Beyond these basics, the Rule points to Cassian's conferences as the guide to the "perfection of the monastic life."

Benedictine monasteries are characterized by many things but most noticeably by the priority of the Divine Office. It is indeed a nourishing and practical framework for a life focused on the spiritual journey. But it is a means not an end. Few Western monasteries teach their novices a way into the prayer of the heart that is the explicit goal of the Orthodox monastery. Fewer still incorporate contemplative prayer as a communal practice.

It could be argued that the Office itself can be prayed contemplatively. There are contemplative dimensions to the liturgy, as Cipriano Vagaggini showed. The Benedictine tradition emphasizes personal *lectio* as well, but generally leaves the rest to the individual monk. The fact that "the rest" is what it's all about is not always made evident to newcomers. There has been a great historical strength in this aiming low. It allowed some individual monks to scale the heights, as Cassian would say. It allowed the monastery to be a place where a wide range of individual temperaments could be welcomed and harmonized and be of service to the Church.

The danger of aiming low on the contemplative scale, however, has been the risk of sloth or acedia. If one does not aim high, it is difficult to climb out of the recurrent bouts of apathy, discouragement, and depression that the Desert Fathers wisely saw as the great enemy of monastic progress. Merton saw this as one of the great spiritual diseases of the modern world. John Climacus called it the "child of talkativeness," presumably meaning not only chatter in the cloister but the result of too many words at prayer. Once the demon of acedia has a grip, it is hard to get free of it. And the danger of a monasticism that does not make contemplation the explicit goal of the monk is that the monastery itself becomes a place of institutionalized acedia.

The great monastic teachers of our time help monks see this in a clearer if more discomforting light than has been possible for a long time. Their witness to the contemplative life of the world shows that the monastery is essentially a place of contemplation, of course. But contemplation means more than atmospherics and liturgical arts. It is the work of the heart as well as the meaning of monastic solitude and escape from the world. Cassian says the monk must climb the mountain of solitude in order to see Christ in his risen glory, no longer after the manner of the flesh.

However, if there are different kinds of monks (not all bad), there will be different kinds of monasteries too. The genius of the Rule is that, through its essential modesty and self-transcendence, it can regulate more than one kind of monastery. It identifies wise practice about the perennial issues that affect us all, both in and outside the monastery: moderation, balance, compassion, authority, community, discipline, basic priorities. Monastic renewal has usually happened when this insight into the priority of contemplation as an inner transformative practice has, at least for some, become stronger than the paralyzing inertia of acedia affecting the many. The great monk teachers of our time have been gripped by this insight as their ancestors were.

Renewing an ancient institution, whether a monastery or a political entity like the British House of Lords, is hard labor. Often the renewal fizzles out after several attempts. Rarely it marks a new lease of life, but the spirit of renewal itself is not crushed by institutional resistance. It simply shifts its center of action.

What Merton, Pennington, Griffiths, and Main represent is the shift of this monastic center toward the wider church, the laity. They remind us that monasticism is essentially a lay mystical movement, calling certain individuals out of the world to represent to the world what its "universal vocation to holiness" means. If their fellow monks can see that what they have done for the world is relevant to the monastic life, there is still hope for renewal and for the flowering, under the banner of St. Benedict, of new forms of monastic life that are truly appropriate for our time.

Apostle to the Laity

Martha F. Krieg

In 1977, I came to the Cistercian Studies Conference in Kalamazoo for the first time. Having received my doctorate the year before, I was delivering one of my first academic papers, and for the first time had left behind my two young daughters. I had never stayed overnight at a conference before. Completely at loose ends, I wandered the halls wondering what to do with myself. A white three-by-five card on a portable bulletin board caught my attention: "A Practical Workshop on the Prayer Technique of *The Cloud of Unknowing*" was to be delivered by Father Basil Pennington in one of the lounges that evening. That sounded more than moderately interesting, since I'd read *The Cloud* and liked it. So I went.

As a Protestant, I'd never met a real monk. None of my preconceptions prepared me for the vivid reality of Father Basil Pennington. Workshop participants were enthusiastically greeted by a tall, large-boned, clean-shaven monk in a striking black and white habit. If this was a monk, and clearly he was, nothing about him seemed stereotypical except the habit. In short order, he gave a brief introduction to Centering Prayer, linking it to Scripture and *The Cloud of Unknowing*, and led us in about fifteen minutes of Centering Prayer, followed by questions and answers.

Two things were obvious: this was a monk who experienced what he was talking about, and whose primary concern in the workshop was to ensure that his listeners understood that the invitation to a deeper relationship with God was aimed at each of them. I left the workshop with the conviction that I had found the source of my attraction to medieval studies: a desire for a relationship with God that permeated all of life in a way that didn't seem to be happening in suburban American Christianity. I didn't know that it was the beginning of twenty-eight years of knowing and growing with Father Basil, of formation through the Cistercian Studies sections at Kalamazoo, journeying with Cistercians to monasteries in Europe, conversion to Catholicism, membership in the Conversi (lay persons) affiliated with New Melleray Abbey, and one of the most serious friendships in my life.

After that first workshop with Father Basil, I did try to practice Centering Prayer. Being a working mother with two (later three) small children, however, "two prayer times a day" never seemed to be available. The idea of centering before supper made perfectly clear to me the difference between living in a monastery where one simply turns up for meals, and being the person making the meals while helping the children with their homework! Nonetheless, something had permanently changed in how I could relate to God. It was as though Father Basil had somehow connected the plug and thrown the switch.

My relationship with God, and my ability to center in tiny, unexpected bits of time continued to grow. When not actively thinking of anything else, I would find the Jesus prayer or the antiphon "O God, come to my assistance; O Lord, make haste to help me" rising to the surface. Finally, about twelve years ago, I began to be able to find time to take a more consistent prayer time, and have been doing so ever since.

I have found that I am not unique in having been affected this way by Father Basil. A request for other people's experiences led to a response from Anita Shaperd, who said:

As a student at Kalamazoo College during the 1970s, I had the opportunity to attend a number of the medieval conferences at Western Michigan University. It was my great fortune that Father Basil gave an unscheduled evening seminar on Centering Prayer at one of them. I would guess that more than one hundred people crowded into one of the student lounges to hear him explain the practice. Looking back, it seems clear that he and his Cistercian colleagues must have invented the form about that time! Whatever it was he said, whatever phase of development the practice was then in, it struck a chord, because I went home and started doing it on a regular basis for quite some time. Eventually, I did stop doing the practice and it was over twenty years before I heard another word about it: four or five years ago, I attended an "Introduction to Centering Prayer" workshop at St. Benedict's Catholic Church in Chicago. It was as though the twenty years away from all things contemplative had never existed, except that Contemplative Outreach and a slew of resources on the topic had been developed in the interim. Many wonderful things have developed in my life since then as a result of my increasing involvement, and I credit Father Basil with all of them, although he and I never exchanged a single word personally.

From my experience and Anita's, I deduce that it would be a mistake to poll people six months or a year after attending a Centering Prayer workshop, only to find they aren't centering twenty minutes each day, and conclude that they derived nothing from the teaching. The seed for both of us was planted quite firmly, and in good soil. It awaited the proper season of life to flower in a more visible way.

Father Basil did not operate alone in teaching Contemplative Prayer. Father William Meninger, OCSO, and Father Thomas Keating, OCSO, also began the teachings and still continue them. Through their joint effort, Contemplative Outreach was formed to enable those they had trained to train others. Contemplative Outreach is active in more than twenty states across the United States, as well as in at least three other countries.

How did Father Basil reach nonmonastic people? There were three main methods. First, for many years he gave workshops at St. Joseph's Abbey in his capacity as vocations director, as well as to retreatants. He also traveled extensively giving workshops on contemplative prayer and *lectio divina*. Second, beginning in 1977 he published a large number of books and articles addressed primarily to nonmonastics. Third, he helped found and run organizations such as Contemplative Outreach and the Mastery Foundation, while also being involved in interreligious dialogue.

When I began to pull together a bibliography of his work, I went through the house pulling his books off the shelves. I was surprised to discover that over the past quarter century and more, I had acquired approximately a book a year. Even more surprising, as I built the list by adding to it the "other books by the same author," it became clear that there were many more, some of which I'd never seen. Cover blurbs, memorial articles following his death, and workshop advertisements referred to his "many book and articles"—but until I delved into the Pennington Archives at Western Michigan University, the full extent of what he had produced had escaped me. Even ignoring the scholarly output, such as translations done for Cistercian Publications and the profusion of articles published in religious journals, he published at least eighty-seven books, several small pamphlets, and numerous articles for newspapers. And he managed to do this while traveling extensively and serving as superior at two monasteries. When asked how he could write so much, his response was, "People ask me how I write so many books, and I say, 'Well, I center several hours a day.'"

The impression that Father Basil was not living a normal version of Cistercian stability would seem to be correct and not simply a result of jealous comments. It was not uncommon for him to lead twelve Centering Prayer workshops outside the abbey in any six-month period, and for a while he traveled outside the United States once or twice a year to lead programs. He seemed at times to be serving as a poster child for the joke inside his community: join the Cistercians, see the world! But all this travel served a real purpose: the edification of the entire Church by the empowering of her children.

Father Basil himself in *Long on the Journey* refers to the fact that sometimes his brother monks found it hard to accept "the monk that I am" and "my gifts—and the way I use them." His writing was often deeply personal. This was the key to making what he said about a true relationship with God believable, but it could appear to be self-aggrandizing. Like St. Bernard before him, sometimes he seemed to spend more time than was profitable for his own peace and stability outside the monastery, and this could be problematic and unpopular. For both St. Bernard and Father Basil, it sometimes seemed to verge on grandstanding rather than authentically preserving the monastic vocation.

How did Father Basil himself feel about traveling so much? Those who lived with him in enclosure can say better than I how well his personality—especially in his vigorous younger days—was suited to perfect, traditional stability. I know from personal discussions with him that he deeply longed to be at Spencer; that he loved it dearly. Traveling to give workshops is at the same time both draining and fulfilling. I suspect he needed a balance between his enclosure and his travel, and that neither alone would have worked well. Certainly those of us who have been profoundly and permanently affected by his ministry deeply appreciate the generosity of the monastic community in allowing him to risk exercising his gifts in these atypical ways.

The Beginning of Centering Prayer

Armand Proulx

The Centering Prayer movement began in 1974. Though born of ancient times, the movement then was a mere child. Three wise men assisted in its birth: Thomas Keating, then abbot of St. Joseph's Abbey in Spencer, Massachusetts; William Meninger, fellow monk, who had read *The Cloud of Unknowing,* the prayer's medieval ancestor, more than 150 times; and Basil Pennington, the gangling missionary monk, who would soon be led to tell the story of the child's birth and to spread its growth to many parts of the world. Within the monastery at Spencer, the child was known as the "Prayer of the Cloud," but within a year it would emerge from the abbey with a new name.

As I remember Basil, another great missionary comes to mind. Paul of Tarsus was his name. Though small in stature, his spirit was large and intense. He circled the known world in his day to spread the gospel message. Basil burned with the same zeal, and seemed to have no choice but to stride the earth to spread the good news of the simple prayer of quiet. He accomplished his mission with larger-than-life exuberance. I only wish that he had survived the one car wreck that took his life in the way Paul survived three shipwrecks.

In 1974, I was serving a second term as the Provincial Superior of the LaSalette Missionaries. I was also deep in the middle of a huge congregation-wide financial crisis when a phone call came from the Conference of Major Superiors of Men. Father Frank Gokey, Edmundite and conference secretary, was on the line.

He had a request: please accept the role of chairperson of the conference's Religious Life committee.

"Can't do it, Frank," was my immediate response. He knew the predicament I was in. Still he persisted. He mentioned how fine a committee I'd be working with. That's when I first heard of Basil Pennington. Some of the other members of the committee were Moses Anderson, future bishop; Thomas Clarke, a highly respected Jesuit theologian, teacher, and writer; and Martin Helldorfer, who would go on to write numerous books and articles on prayer and the spirituality of work. I finally accepted. In retrospect, that call and my response proved to be a personal tipping moment of the greatest significance. I can't imagine what my life and my ministry would be like if I had not finally said yes to what, at the time, seemed an impossible request.

The committee met in Chicago and that is where I first met Basil. It was actually a joint meeting of two committees: the committee on the Ecclesial Role of Women from the Leadership Conference of Women Religious and our Religious Life committee. Basil came into the meeting room crackling with high energy. Though in his forties, his name and his large frame combined to make him look venerable beyond his years, an impressive figure stepping out of both the Hebrew Bible and the New Testament.

Soon he was sharing a vision and a pressing concern. The concern was for the leaders of religious congregations who at the time were struggling through the changes mandated by Vatican II and the exodus of members that had begun in the late 1960s. They were burning out. They needed to tap into a new and deeper source of energy, he said. They needed to know where to go for deep soul refreshment.

The time for the presentation of the child to the world had arrived. Contemplation, as far as the three wise men and their community in Spencer were concerned, was an idea whose time was long overdue. Enter the vision: a simple prayer that would lead these tired leaders to the living waters of God's grace.

The meeting quickly turned logistical. Let there be an ad hoc committee to launch the teaching of the Prayer of the Cloud! It was time, as it were, for the child to go to Jerusalem. And so it came to pass, that less than two months after the meeting in Chicago, Sister Kieran Flynn of the Sisters of Mercy of Providence, Rhode Island, and I met with Basil to craft a contemplative workshop format and agenda. It was at this first workshop, in a seamless moment, that the Prayer of the Cloud got a new name. This is how Basil described what happened in an article years later:

> *Centering Prayer*—the name has certainly caught on. I can remember well when it first began to be used. It was at the first prayer shop we did outside the monastic retreat house. There was a team working with me. In the course of this initial prayer shop I quoted Thomas Merton frequently, using such quotations as "The best way to come to God is to go to your own center and pass through to the center into the center of God." Father Armand Proulx, Provincial Superior of the LaSalette Fathers, began to call our "Prayer of the Cloud" "Centering Prayer." Our traditional little method came home from the prayershop with a new name.
>
> (From Basil's introduction to Centering Prayer in *Daily Life and Ministry*. Edited by Gustave Reininger. New York: Continuum, 1998.)

The post-workshop debriefing also yielded a simpler format, which we took to the second Centering Prayer workshop at a retreat house along the bayous near New Orleans. As at the first workshop, there were no printed handouts. But there was Basil.

He gathered the twenty or so participants, spelled out the three rules that every Centering Prayer practitioner knows by heart, offered a prayer of consent to the presence and action of God within, slipped into silence for twenty minutes with the rest of us, then emerged from the deep quiet with a slow, deliberate recitation of the Our Father. Questions and reflections followed. We repeated this simple rhythmic unit twice more during the first day of the workshop, and once during the second morning, closing before lunch with the celebration of the Eucharist. Moses Anderson participated in this second workshop. I can still hear his powerful, soulful rendition of *Let Us Break Bread Together* during the sharing of the bread and cup.

The next significant stop on the mission to take Centering Prayer still further beyond the monastery walls was at the annual meeting of the Conference of Major Superiors of Men in New Orleans in August of 1975. Early afternoon of the first day, Basil told the Centering Prayer story, situated it within the history of the contemplative tradition, invited a sister, a priest, and a brother on stage to share how Centering Prayer had enriched their lives, and then proceeded to lead the assembly in a twenty-minute contemplative practice. Toward evening, Abbot Thomas Keating celebrated the Eucharist. The period of deep silence in the auditorium and the gathering of the assembly around the table highlighted the annual meeting and gave powerful impetus to the movement.

Next on Basil's missionary journey was a third Centering Prayer workshop, this time in Plano, Illinois, later the same year. These initial "prayer shops" and the annual meeting in New Orleans, along with a series of instructional tapes and Centering Prayer sessions William Meninger began offering at the monastery, constituted the oral launching of the Centering Prayer movement.

Then, like the letter writers of the apostolic era, Thomas Keating, Thomas Clarke, William Meninger, and Basil began writing "letters" concerning the centering way. The first book on the subject, *Finding Grace at the Center,* appeared in 1978. It was based on four articles that had appeared in various religious publications in 1977 and 1978: "Centering Prayer—Prayer of Quiet," by Basil; "Cultivating the Centering Prayer" and "Contemplative Prayer in the Christian Tradition: An Historical Perspective," by Thomas Keating; and "Finding Grace at the Center," by Thomas Clarke. The book also listed twenty retreat centers and several Centering Prayer teachers, who had been trained by Father Meninger, Thomas Keating, or Basil. Thus it was that, in three short years, from 1975 to 1978, through workshops, retreats, articles, tapes, and books, the child came of age.

By 1981, I had left the priesthood, but I stayed in touch with Basil through the years. We had lunch together shortly before the fatal car accident. Following in the footsteps of my friend and mentor, I press forward with the same concern and vision Basil brought to that launching meeting in Chicago thirty-two years ago.

Three years ago, I became pastor of the Second Congregational Church in Greenfield, Massachusetts. Shortly after my arrival, three Centering Prayer groups formed and still meet once a week to share Scripture and silence. This ministry of silence has extended beyond the church, as we offer Centering Prayer workshops for clergy and laity.

Greenfield is situated in the Pioneer Valley along the Connecticut River, the site of one of the Great Awakenings that occurred under the powerful voices of preachers who urged the faithful to "gather by the river." I see the Centering Prayer movement as a Quiet Awakening where the call is for us to go to the wellspring of our own hearts. This spring, Father Keating will come to our church on the common to issue again that call. We expect a huge crowd. People will come from up and down the valley and from the hills beyond the river to hear him speak on "Centering Prayer, Deep Healing for the Soul." It will be an opportunity for me to thank one of the three wise men who in the beginning came bearing a most precious gift.

Personal Encounter with
Basil Pennington

Grace Padilla

As I look back, I realize it was God's mercy and compassion that led me to Basil. In July 1984, I was undergoing what my spiritual confessor called "a desert experience." Nothing seemed to make sense to me. In desperation one afternoon, I asked my daughter to drop me at the Catholic bookstore on her way to class.

Time passed so quickly I panicked when, after four hours, I saw my daughter tooting the horn of her car. I couldn't go home empty-handed, so I grabbed the book closest to me and paid for it. Some time later, I read the book. I was in such a state that I could not find consolation in anything. Mass was simply something to pass the time. Books were simply meaningless words. Even praying was an ordeal. Nonetheless, I persevered with my prayers, going to Mass daily, and tried to read.

Eventually, I remembered the book I had purchased two weeks earlier. It was still in the back of the car. For the first time, I saw the title: *Centering Prayer: Renewing an Ancient Christian Prayer Form* by M. Basil Pennington. This book made sense to me. I found I could pray without being apprehensive. During Centering Prayer, I forgot self and focused my attention on God. Slowly a veil lifted and once again I began to hope.

I took to Centering Prayer like a duck to water. The transformation in my life seemed instantaneous. Life started to have meaning once more. I became a woman obsessed with the prayer and shared it with some of my closest friends in the parish. Whenever I had an opportunity to talk with anyone, it was about Centering Prayer. My parish priest, Father Hugh Zurat, OFM, was very encouraging. He helped me gather the parishioners, and even consented to my having a prayer room. This was a dream come true, since I had asked him for this before to no avail. Already the power of the prayer was starting to make itself felt.

Gratefully I wrote to Father Basil, and I got an immediate response! I was soon to find out that this sort of hospitality was second nature to him. He was always warm and amiable, and every person was precious to him. The next year, on my annual visit to my children in Connecticut, I made the first of many grace-filled visits to Spencer, Massachusetts, less than an hour away.

The following year, I attended my first workshop with Father Basil in Redwood City, California. His last talk at the retreat was on the transfiguration with the phrase: "Tell no one about the vision until the Son of man has risen from the dead" (Mt. 17:9). Then I heard him continue—"But the Son of man has risen—go proclaim him to everyone. Teach them the prayer that they may come to an experience of him!"

As though something ominous was being asked of me, I leaned back shaking, and in my head I heard—*Me, talk to a crowd! Never!* I would not even volunteer to lead the Our Father. I would get so nervous I would forget parts of it. *Lord, I am so sorry to let you down.* Never! Never! Never! I trembled, convinced it was an impossibility, yet fearful there might even be the slightest possibility. *Never!* I said to myself once again.

My fear of talking to groups would not go away, but I finally solved that problem by purchasing a set of Father Basil's tapes on Centering Prayer. During our weekly Centering Prayer sessions, I would play part of a tape and ask the group to reflect on it. Thus began my Centering Prayer ministry.

I was oblivious to the fact that the Holy Spirit was working double time. Just recently I heard from Father Hugh about the Centering Prayer movement in the parish:

> As far as Centering Prayer was concerned, if I remember rightly, for me it was tied with parish renewal. For any kind of conversion experience to be "successful" (who can really measure success except he who reads the hearts of all?), there is a need for a strong prayer base. That is why praying was such an integral part of the parish renewal process. I was concerned about this and so when you came with your proposal regarding Centering Prayer, this was a prayer being answered. I was more than willing to see it started, without ever realizing how it would develop— truly the work of the Lord. The rest is history. Centering Prayer was another part of God's comprehensive plan for our parish and beyond. We were used, and we should be extremely grateful for that.

Demands for Centering Prayer workshops in the Philippines started coming in. I had a very dear friend Araceli Santos who, like me, is a Secular Franciscan. She had attended the workshop in Redwood City with me in 1986. She and I presented the workshops and divided the talking between us. I was always anxious and apprehensive every time I had to give a talk and was thankful for Cely's courage and encouragement.

In one of my visits to Father Basil in Spencer, I told him a group had asked me to give a talk on Centering Prayer and expected me to do it in thirty minutes. He burst into laughter and said, "That should be no problem—talk about the prayer for ten minutes and do the prayer for twenty minutes." That was the first time he referred to his KISS principle—"Keep it simple, sweetheart"! His no-nonsense attitude about it gave me the courage to share the prayer. I quickly learned that doing the prayer was much more valuable than talking about it.

Each year I went to the States, and I made a point of visiting Spencer. Each time, I invited Father Basil to come to the Philippines. On my third or fourth visit, he told me it was a possibility. I was beside myself with joy. Father Basil coming to the Philippines!

Then reality set in. What am I going to do? Who can I invite to come? Where will it be held? I don't remember now how it all came together, I only remember how many people were interested in deepening their prayer life and eager to listen to Father Basil. Undoubtedly his fame had preceded him. Mercifully I wasn't aware I was dealing with one of the great spiritual mentors of our time. I would have been totally starstruck and completely immobilized. As I look back, I realize the Holy Spirit was working all along.

On his first visit in 1987, I arranged for him to meet with Cardinal Jaime L. Sin, Archbishop of Manila. He asked Father Basil to give a talk to his priests. At the end of the session, one priest came up and told him, "I came with serious doubts about continuing my priesthood, but I leave so inspired and encouraged to go on." Father Basil later said, "For this alone, my visit to the Philippines was well worth it."

Along with Centering Prayer, Father Basil and I talked a lot about *lectio divina*. *Lectio*, as we often called it, played a profoundly important role in Father's life. *Lectio* is an experiential hearing of the Word of God. To attain a total open listening to the Word, we need to dip again and again into the divine reading through *lectio divina*. One afternoon our conversation about *lectio* got so animated, I burst out saying, "Father, you should write a book on *lectio* similar to the way you have with Centering Prayer."

Another day at a workshop, Father Basil said, "Our inner attitude—the listening that we are—will make all the difference in our ability to hear what God is telling us." "The listening that we are"—how quaintly said, yet it seemed to portend something elusive, something I needed to plumb the meaning of.

I took advantage of a beautiful afternoon, sitting under one of those trees near the guesthouse in Spencer to ask him more about it. "Each of us is a certain listening, a certain openness to being, to reality, to communication," he said. Then he continued:

> Everything that has been a part of our lives since the moment of our creation has had its role in shaping the listening that we are. It is good for us to realize that we are a certain, definable listening. It is as though my listening has a physical shape to it. As things come across my listening, I get only what falls within the parameters of the listening that I am.

I pressed Father to explain further. He went on,

> Everything we perceive comes through the filters of the listening we are. It is important to realize and accept that I am a certain limited listening. If I am a very "set" person, very rigid in my ideas and convictions, that is it. That is all I get and all I will ever get. On the other hand, if I am a very open person, then each thing I encounter in my "listening" has the potential to expand my listening, to push out my boundaries perhaps just a little bit more.

I drove back to Connecticut reflecting on "the listening that we are." That afternoon was firmly etched in my mind for interiorly I took a stand to continually be conscious of the listening I am in my relationships as wife, mother, sister, friend, and most especially as "one who sits daily at the foot of the Master."

Father did get to write the book *Lectio Divina: Renewing the Ancient Practice of Praying the Scripture*, which paralleled his book *Centering Prayer: Renewing an Ancient Christian Prayer Form*. I shall never forget the morning he gave me a copy. I was leaving the next day, and he suggested meeting for breakfast. I was beside myself with joy to be able to see him once more. Father had that extraordinary ability to make you feel so special, so important—he was truly a person who personified love. He said he would be a little late because he had to say Mass, but I was to go directly to what was referred to as the Ethan Allen House, near the gift shop, and he would meet me there after Mass.

I remember it was a cold morning late in autumn. As I entered the cottage, it felt so warm and inviting. I could smell the coffee percolating and some sausages slowly cooking on a grill. The whole atmosphere spoke of the man—warm, loving, inviting, joyful, and peaceful. But all that was nothing compared to his presence as he bounced into the room, his deep blue eyes crinkling into smiles of pure joy, his arms open wide with a warm hug, and his ready smile so spontaneous and delightful. For a split second I thought, "I saw the face of God and lived!" I am sure many of you who have met him felt this way too.

All through breakfast he seemed so interested with everything that had happened since we last saw each other. After an hour, as I stood to say my good-bye, he gave me a couple of books. He had a book for me every time I visited him. "Oh Father, you wrote the book on *lectio*!" "As promised. . . ." came the reply. He was smiling—but his smile seemed to convey *There is more to come.* On the dedication page was printed: "For Michael a true Christian gentleman, a friend, a brother, a true lover of *lectio,* and for Grace and all those with whom I had the privilege of sharing Centering Prayer." My joy was full to overflowing.

Father Basil introduced me to some powerful excercises that left a deep impression on me. At the end of one of his earlier retreats, he instructed us to form a line. We were each to come forward to make a stand on what we wanted to be.

Father Basil went on to explain. "We want to define ourselves in ways that open the space for us to live up to our fullest potential and beyond. I may be painfully aware that I often become angry and express myself in this way. I can take a stand and declare: I am a kind and gentle person. And with that declaration, I open the space for me to live up to that declaration."

This seemed to touch a sensitive cord within me. Quite often, we devalue ourselves. Deep down we don't think much of ourselves despite appearances to the contrary. Sometimes we overcompensate to hide the our low self-image, and we appear to be always in control and controlling. I made a mental note of how often I said, "I am shy." "I have no talent." "I am just content to be a follower." "I can't talk." I wondered if these were cop-out statements for not wanting to initiate anything or to be responsible. Yet in my own quiet way, I was arrogantly critical and opinionated.

We can begin to notice the way we define ourselves, either aloud or just to ourselves. We can decide if we like these definitions or if we want to change. We can best wipe out limiting definitions by making new declarations wherein we take a stand to be just the opposite. Taking a stand opens up the space for us to live up to our true potential.

Besides general attitudes, we can take a stand and make declarations in regard to particular elements of our lives: I am a person who sits each day at the feet of my Lord and listens to him in his inspired Word. I am a person who each day sits in silent meditation allowing the Lord to refresh me. When I take a stand and make a declaration, the very truth of my being calls me forth to live up to who I say that I am. The space is opened, and I am empowered to live up to it. I did make a stand that afternoon and to this day I have made it the vision and mission of my life. I went up to Father Basil and said, "I am a sacrament of God's love."

I have a letter from my friend Billie Trinidad, describing her reaction at the same workshop.

———————

Dearest Grace,

Seeing Father Basil's picture reminded me of the circumstances of how we met. Do you remember? You and I were communicating by phone and had never met face to face. If you remember, I almost didn't go to that talk by Father, because all my companions couldn't come. But you promised to be there and so I went. And I met a truly gentle man, so full of the love of the Lord. He always seemed to have a smile on his face, but his eyes were the ones that expressed the smile more than just his lips.

I will never forget the stand that he had us all take that day. It really wasn't clear to me what it meant to make a stand. All I could remember was that it wasn't supposed to begin with the words, "I will try." Instead it was a statement of fact, a statement that sort of takes over our lives and somehow influences the way we live.

And so I made a stand; without thinking, I stood up and said, "My stand is that my life will be a constant yes to God." And the minute I expressed it, I felt the power of my words and the sanctity of my stand, most especially because Father Basil was standing right in front of me. You remember, I ran to the bathroom to throw up!

How far that stand was to take me, I had no idea. It is something that comes back to me again and again when I need a gentle reminder when things seem to fall apart and lose their relevance and meaning. It is an anchor that holds me and keeps me connected.

My enthusiasm to teach Centering Prayer did not match my ability to teach the prayer. While I would readily talk of Centering Prayer with people one-on-one, the idea of standing before crowds challenged me beyond endurance. I brought this up with Father Basil. He burst into a hearty laughter and simply left me with a question to ponder, "Why you are fearful; you of little faith?"

A question to answer another question was no answer for me! When I pressed him to explain further, his deep blue eyes broke into an impish smile, but he refused to elaborate. I stayed with the question until our visit the following year. I was surprised what came up when I was left with a question. It challenged my priorities and my motivations. Although the fear was still there, the determination to teach Centering Prayer solidified. I had the perfect venue for it, the Catholic Women's League of the Philippines, an organization for women with a membership of 250,000, of which I was a board member.

The following year, I shared with Father Basil what surfaced with the question he left me. It was then that Father talked to me about living the question. "It is good to live in the question," Father Basil went on to say:

A pat answer is closed. It is finished. That's all there is to it. It goes nowhere and leaves little room for hope. A question opens space for us. It is full of possibility.

It is paradoxical how much living in a question can bring clarity to our present experience. We see everything in a new perspective. We plumb the meaning of each thing more deeply. Each relationship takes on more meaning. We look at each of the loved ones around us and sense the preciousness of our relationship with them, how beautiful they are, even with all their faults, all those little things that so annoy us. The elements of our daily routine have more meaning; we enjoy them with a sense of wholeness.

Before I left, Father Basil presented me with a book, *Living in the Question*. In it he wrote, "May the Great Answer fill your life with boundless love and joy." Basil gave me many books he authored over the years; this is one of those I treasure most.

REFLECTION

Gerry O'Rourke

While I feel very honored to write about my friend and colleague Basil Pennington, there is also a reluctance I have only been able to articulate after weeks of hesitation. It has to do with a nagging thought that I should have gone first and it should have been Basil's job to do this for me! Until now, I had not really let go of him and given him permission to leave us and go to the God that he loved so much.

You see, I always thought Basil would outlive me and be part of my life. I always thought that he would be in his beloved monastery at Spencer or in one of the many worldwide monasteries that sought his counsel and his presence. Or at least, I thought, he would be on a plane that would pass through San Francisco, and I would be honored to take him to an elegant San Francisco restaurant for a meal.

For me, Basil was a giant of a man. Wherever he was—monastic chapel, conference room, cathedral, or some more modest meeting room—he brought with him a presence of peace, of spirituality, of inclusion, of excitement, of anticipation, and always with a truly gentle touch.

Most of our relationship was sourced in our creation and development of the Mastery Foundation. We both were blessed to be among the cofounders, and an immediate gift resulting from that work was the creation of a relationship among the dozen of us at the beginning—working together in a spirit of total trust, unity, acknowledgment, and appreciation. It was a space of unity across many denominational and religious differences. It was and still is a miraculous space of peace and harmony.

Father Basil's presence brought instant recognition of our work and intentions. His fearless public acknowledgment gave our work an immediate authority. Those were not small things in a world that then knew little or nothing about inter-religious harmony and working together.

Of course his greatest and longest lasting gift to us, and certainly to me personally, was Centering Prayer. Looking back to 1983 and the noisy jangled world we have lived in since, Centering Prayer could not have been more timely.

In my seminary training at St. Patrick's, in Maynooth, Ireland, I was introduced to the term "contemplative prayer." In our ascetical theology classes, seminarian candidates for the secular or diocesan priesthood were told that contemplative prayer was not for us. It was for the great contemplative orders in the Church like Father Basil's Cistercians or the Orthodox monks in places like Mount Athos.

Then along came Father Basil who, with the approval of the Vatican, openly declared that contemplative prayer is for everybody. He called it Centering Prayer. It is a divinely inspired title, a title that declares the possibility that this prayer of silence is available to both the laity and the ordained, those of all denominations, religions, and spiritualities. In Father Basil's universal vision of God's love at work in our world, he saw the grace of Centering Prayer as the place we can all come together in silence with the peace and harmony we long for and need in our troubled world.

May Father Basil's love and vision continue to bless and enlighten us all. May his spirit continue to inflame our hearts with the gentle love that always flowed to us from his great heart. May he live into eternity in the space of the unconditional love of God that he manifested for us while he was with us in this passing life.

Centering Prayer and Salesian Spirituality: Connections

Lewis S. Fiorelli, OSFS

My friendship with Basil Pennington extended over three decades and while it is not part of my daily practice, I count myself as a witness to the transforming power of Centering Prayer in many lives.

At every meeting with Basil, I was deeply impressed by the genuineness of his Christian charity and the sincerity of his basic human goodness. Readily and easily, his love embraced everyone who crossed his path in life. Even now, I cannot think of him without a smile on my face and a certain warm feeling in my heart. With his impressive height, ample girth, sparkling blue eyes and ready smile, all coupled with that full snow-white beard, I also can never think of him without at the same time thinking of Santa Claus. And when he wrapped those massive arms around you in a bear hug of a greeting, you knew that you were experiencing firsthand something of the breadth and depth, as well as the ready acceptance, of divine love.

As a friend of Basil and a member of a religious congregation dedicated to living and fostering the spirit and doctrine of St. Francis de Sales, I have often looked for connections between the two men, especially in the area of prayer. Here, I will discuss several of those connections.

Centering Prayer is probably the best-known contemporary expression of praying in the apophatic tradition of the thirteenth-century spiritual masterpiece, *The Cloud of Unknowing*. The starting point for prayer in the apophatic tradition is the total otherness of God, the complete transcendence of the Creator to creation. As pure spirit, God lies utterly beyond the finite limits of the human being and cannot therefore be conceived or imagined by human thought. In this tradition, one prays without words, concepts, or images. The mind is stilled and the spirit quieted. While praying, one surrenders in faith to the bright darkness of the cloud of unknowing, content simply to be in the presence of God who is knowable only to himself.

Prayer in the Salesian tradition, on the other hand, is deeply rooted in the kataphatic tradition to which, because of his long familiarity with the Ignatian tradition, St. Francis de Sales was particularly partial. The starting point for prayer in the kataphatic tradition is the immanence of the Creator to his creation in the saving history of the Chosen People and in the Incarnation of the divine Word. This tradition welcomes the fact that, through grace, God has freely chosen to bridge the infinite chasm between himself and his creation. In Jesus, God became flesh and dwelt among us with a truly human face. Thus, this prayer tradition affirms that the human spirit can know something of God by meditating upon the biblical Jesus. One who prays in this tradition actively employs human imagination to the life and person of Jesus with the goal of imitating his relational life with God and neighbor.

Are there connections between prayer in the apophatic tradition and prayer in the kataphatic tradition? I believe there are, and that the development and influence of the prayer life of Francis's spiritual friend and fellow saint, Jane de Chantal, is a wonderful example.

Francis de Sales and Jane de Chantal met for the first time in 1604. She was a recent widow and mother of four young children, and he was already a bishop, and a much sought-after preacher and spiritual guide. Until his death eighteen years later in 1622, their spiritual friendship developed and deepened, and they continued to encourage and support one another in their common pursuit of perfection. Arguably, their greatest collaborative effort was the foundation of a new religious order in 1610, the Visitation of Holy Mary, while the richness of Salesian spirituality is the enduring fruit of their celebrated friendship.

In the area of prayer, it was Jane who led the way in the experience of contemplative prayer. In all likelihood, she was the principal impetus to its increasing prominence in the spiritual writings of Francis. The development of Jane's prayer seems to have had a great influence on Francis and his teachings.

During the first months of their spiritual friendship, Jane sought advice from Francis on prayer. A friend had begun to encourage her to leave behind the discursive form of prayer that Francis had recommended and to pursue contemplative prayer, avoiding the use of "the imagination or understanding." Naturally, Jane sought Francis's advice since he had strongly advocated the use of both.

In his response, Francis acknowledged that while imageless prayer is perhaps appropriate for "those who are already far advanced along the mountain of perfection," for beginners like Jane "who are still in the valleys," the use of "all our faculties, including the imagination," is the surer approach. Docile to the advice of her spiritual guide, Jane faithfully dedicated herself to an hour of daily meditation on the life of Jesus and the mysteries of the faith.

In a short time, however, she began to be drawn strongly to the decidedly more contemplative and apophatic prayer form that she later refers to as "simple attentiveness" or "simple entrustment to God." A "virtually imageless and wordless type of prayer," it came quite naturally to Jane, and it was the prayer that "she identified throughout her life as most uniquely her own." Almost from the beginning, it became "the inner charism of the Order of the Visitation."

Jane describes the prayer this way: "When the time comes to present ourselves before His divine Goodness to speak to Him face to face, which we call prayer, simply the presence of our spirit before His and His before ours forms prayer whether or not we have fine thoughts or feelings. . . . He is touched with the prayer of a soul so simple, humble and surrendered to His will."

While Francis clearly prefers that those who are new to the devout life begin their prayer life "in the valleys" of meditation on the life of Jesus, he writes perceptively in the *Treatise on the Love of God* [1616] of the differences between meditation and contemplation and describes—in a manner that strongly suggests personal experience—a number of contemplative prayer forms. Apparently the experiences of his trusted spiritual friend broadened and deepened this spiritual master's own understanding and experience of the depths and richness of contemplative prayer.

In the final chapters of Book V of the *Treatise*, Francis develops the prayer of praise, a treatment that, while it begins with the kataphatic prayer of praise, ends with the apophatic prayer that he calls "sacred silence" and "unvoiced awe." Wordless and imageless, creation falls silent before God, satisfied to let God praise himself.

My long friendship with Basil Pennington prompted me to look for connections between the apophatic tradition of Centering Prayer and the Salesian teaching on prayer. In the *Treatise on the Love of God*, St. Francis de Sales uses a bold and striking image to note the intimate connection between prayer and life. He writes there that we "conceive" in prayer what we later "bring forth" in life and action. Just as conception is inexorably oriented to the birth that follows, prayer unfailingly bears fruit in one's daily life with others.

No matter how ordinary the circumstance or how fleeting the encounter, whenever I met Father Basil I found in him the same special kindness, warmth, and fire. There was always a ready and welcoming smile on his face and a kind and caring word on his lips. From one visit to another, no matter the length of time between them, he unfailingly remembered and reaffirmed the connections between us.

Even though that good and zealous man must have encountered thousands of people in his full and selfless life, if my experience is typical, he invariably interacted with every one of them as irreplaceably unique and special. One was simply a better person for having been with him even a short while.

I believe that something of the fruitfulness of that good man's prayer life passed from him to me in our every meeting. In his daily and wordless encounters with God through Centering Prayer and *lectio divina*, he surely conceived the good that he was then able to share with such easy grace. Each of us who had the privilege to call Father Basil "friend" was blessed and bettered by the fruit of that man's prayer, a prayer that was daily centered, in the darkness of faith, on the holy and living God.

REFLECTION

Stephen J. Boccuzzi

My contemplative journey began in 1977 when I met Michael Moran and Father Lewis Fiorelli while attending graduate school at The Catholic University of America in Washington, DC. The three of us quickly became spiritual friends and met every week with other colleagues over coffee and conversation. Through this fellowship and sharing, each of us was eventually introduced to the Cistercian spiritual tradition.

That year of spiritual friendship and sharing was a seminal event in my personal spiritual journey. Later that year, Michael would come to know and lead me to meet another special friend, Father Basil Pennington, who would introduce me to Centering Prayer and *lectio divina*.

My spiritual journey would be blessed with another formative experience in 1979 when Michael Moran and I would visit Father Basil at "The Cottage" at St. Joseph's Abbey in Spencer, Massachusetts. During that retreat, I had the good fortune to be instructed on Centering Prayer by Father Basil himself. Years later, I would come to understand that during this retreat the Holy Spirit had ignited within me a special contemplative spirituality that would impact my life and ministries well beyond anything I could have imagined. For me, Father Basil was a spiritual craftsman who, throughout his ministry, used and shared a very special and diverse spiritual toolbox and, in so doing, selflessly helped all those he encountered on their spiritual journey.

Over the years, I crossed paths with Father Basil during periodic retreats or during his enroute visits on his way to a meeting, lecture, or retreat. His unexpected phone calls announcing he would be stopping by were always welcome. These visits expanded over the years to include my family. It was not uncommon for my parents to find him at the front door with another monk in tow. These were special gatherings where we provided food for the body and Basil provided food for the soul. He always embraced us with unrestrained love and always left us more grounded in God's message of love. In many ways he was like a modern-day Jesus, showing up at our homes much like the Lord showed up at the homes of Lazarus, Martha, Mary, and others.

Through the Cistercian experiences provided to me by Father Basil, I have come to believe that within many of us lives a monk, a contemplative who yearns to live simply, in pursuit of communion with God. Distractions and emotions can create a veil that mask the essence of who we truly are. Father Basil's special gift of introducing me to contemplative ways and especially Centering Prayer did not provide an easy road to follow because it brought with it the continual yet rewarding challenges related to confronting the false self, embracing the true self, and most importantly knowing, loving, and serving God. By finding and knowing the monk that lives within my center, where God dwells, I found that I could refresh, renew, and revitalize myself.

In reality our journey is not that different from those who are called to the religious life, including those who follow the monastic traditions. The major difference is that their vocation has called them to serve in a life devoid of the usual distractions of the outside world. But for all of us, it is inevitable that the noise of life will cause us to get off track at times. Knowing the monk that lives within can help to get us back on track.

Father Basil's tremendous gift to humankind has been making accessible tools to help us remain patient and centered. His writings and teachings on Centering Prayer and *lectio divina* make available the richness of monastic spirituality to those living in the hustle and bustle of the modern world.

During one of my visits to the monastery, I remember engaging Father Basil in a discussion about *lectio divina* and my trouble incorporating Scripture into my daily routine. He shared with me an approach that has remained with me and continues to provide richness as I engage with Sripture in my daily life. He suggested that when I read Scripture that I listen for a simple message and reduce what I hear to a single word. For years, this simple advice has served me well.

Recently, I faced a number of serious medical challenges. I struggled terribly with my loss of independence and was consumed with anger and despair. For weeks I sang the "Why me?" chant as my journey was unclear, and I was filled with tremendous anxiety and confusion. During these months, praying at my center was a constant challenge and often all I could do was offer my prayer of pain and distraction. Centering Prayer was and is a tremendous source of grace and strength for me as I continue my journey, hopefully healed of my bodily infirmity.

I was truly blessed to have known Father Basil and to have my life enriched by Centering Prayer and *lectio divina*. I never could have anticipated then how the lessons he taught me and the tools he gave me would serve me over these past years.

Part Four

DREAMER AND CREATOR

Free to Love
The Dreamer and the Realist

E. Glenn Hinson

At the funeral Mass for Father Basil Pennington, his longtime friend and mentor, Father Thomas Keating, observed, "He wanted so much to love everybody he met, but not everybody was responsive. And it must be said that sometimes his love was a little overpowering."

I won't try to assess the second part of the remark except to wonder whether the problem of overpowering rested in Basil or in a culture, perhaps with some legitimacy, grown suspicious of false and deceptive loves, of people wanting love but afraid lest they again fall prey to exploitation. Because we are pressed in on every side by "wolves in sheep's clothing," we find it hard to trust a genuine embodier of the love of God. Only the naive, we judge, could believe anyone would act out of such unselfish motives. Check Jesus as exhibit A of one who came to his own and his own did not accept him (Jn. 1:11).

I want to focus, however, on what lay behind Basil's ardent desire "to love everybody he met." I have no facts and figures to confirm Father Keating's observation, but it resonates with what I have experienced in more than thirty years of friendship with Father Pennington. From the first time I met him at a gathering of the Ecumenical Institute of Spirituality at Wainwright House in New York in 1973, I have thought Basil Pennington tried to live out this line from William Blake: "We are put on earth for a little space that we may learn to bear the beams of love."

Perhaps none of us really knows how best "to bear the beams of love," but if it is possible for human beings to beam love energies toward other persons, this gentle giant did so. His smiles and hugs radiated warmth and welcome. Indeed, a Clarist sister once charged that his writings didn't "convey the love and warmth that is in his face." Basil responded to her letter by determining to let his writing "flow more naturally and directly from my heart to the reader whom I love." What his personal mien suggested, he translated into hospitality and generosity. Thanks to that spirit, for instance, Trappist monasteries—St. Joseph's in Spencer, Massachusetts; Holy Spirit in Conyers, Georgia; Holy Cross in Berryville, Virginia; and Gethemani near Bardstown, Kentucky—hosted the Ecumenical Institute of Spirituality repeatedly. Thanks to it, too, I received complimentary copies of virtually every book Father Pennington wrote or edited since we first met. He loved with the same kind of extravagance Jesus attributed to the loving Father of his great parable of the prodigal son (Lk. 15:11–32).

How do we account for such reckless expenditure of love or, more precisely, a person so imbued with desire to love everyone he met? In the final analysis one might say what Claude Montefiore said at the death of Baron Friedrich von Hügel: "Souls like that, one has to have God to account for them."

Father Pennington himself would have ascribed any of the redeeming qualities he possessed to the Holy Spirit. The Spirit is "the effective presence of God's great love for us," he noted in one journal. "The Spirit is love—divine love personified; all the love of the Father for the Son and of the Son for the Father," he reflected later. "And now that love is mine. So I am loved. And so can I love. . . . On each one I meet today I can pour out the fullness of divine Love with all his healing and affirmation." Bearing the beams of love like Basil Pennington did, however, does not just happen. Something must condition those who would love as God loves.

The first place to look for a source is in the Trappist community in which Basil spent most of his life. Bernard of Clairvaux called the Cistercian monastery "a school of love," and that is what it proved to be for Basil Pennington as it did for a badly scarred youth like Thomas Merton, who became the pioneer and polestar for Basil and many other Trappists. Basil judged that the most important monastic value for him and for the monastery he resided in was whether "our monastic life [is] truly a school of love, true love, the love who is the Holy Spirit and our participation in that love" and whether it is "lived in such wise that church and society not only receive it but can experience it."

One could hardly reach any other conclusion from his own writings and activities than that Basil Pennington really experienced love there and was straining every fiber of his being to enable both church and society to do the same. What in this simple way of living could have had such an effect?

The Rule of Benedict laid out a pattern for life that could effect a "conversion of life and manners." The monks' day would consist of three parts: about three or four hours gathering as a community to recite the psalms eight times a day; three or four hours of *lectio divina*, chiefly individual reading and meditating on Scriptures and praying; and six hours of manual or other labor conducted in attentive silence. Such a regimen did not work for everyone, but for persons called to the vocation of prayer it often did result in profound transformation, above all, to love. Thomas Merton, who entered Gethsemani a sad and world-weary youth, exulted after almost seven years in this "school of love":

Loves sails me around the house. I walk two steps on the ground and four steps in the air. It is love. It is consolation. I don't care if it is consolation. I am not attached to consolation. I love God. Love carries me all around. I don't want to do anything but love. And when the bell rings it is like pulling teeth to make myself shift because of that love, secret love, hidden love, obscure love, down inside me and outside me where I don't care to talk about it. Anyway I don't have the time or the energy to discuss such matters. I have only time for eternity, which is to say for love, love, love. Maybe Saint Teresa would like to have me snap out of it but it is pure, I tell you; I am not attached to it (I hope) and it is love and it gives me soft punches all the time in the center of my heart. Love is pushing me around the monastery, love is kicking me all around like a gong I tell you, love is the only thing that makes it possible for me to continue to tick.

(Thomas Merton, *The Sign of Jonas*)

Merton would come down to earth very shortly under his new abbot, James Fox, as his celebrity status that came with the publication of *The Seven Storey Mountain* and his ordination to the priesthood radically altered his life in the monastery. But he never gave up his stout conviction that love is at the heart of things. What changed was a broadening and expanding of love to encompass not only God and his brothers at Gethsemani but also the "world" he had thought he could leave behind when he entered. Basil Pennington, who entered St. Joseph's about the time Merton entered those words in his journal, was one of Merton's most apt and enthusiastic disciples who could embody and broadcast the gospel of love far and wide.

To understand more clearly how the Benedictine regimen generates lovers, however, we need to look more closely at one aspect to which, judging by his writings, Basil Pennington applied himself most assiduously. Father Pennington, like Father Keating, gained an international reputation for his teaching and writing about a special form of prayer developed especially by Thomas Merton, Centering Prayer. In his own perspective and practice, however, Father Pennington placed centering within the context of *lectio divina*. "I look forward every day to meeting the Lord in *lectio*," he said in a late writing. "It is a time of intimacy, of heart to heart. We know the Lord is truly present in his inspired Word." Elsewhere, he advised, "It is well to keep the sacred Scriptures enthroned in our home in a place of honor as a Real Presence of the Word in our midst." A number of his writings consist of selections from Scripture with his brief meditations.

Lectio divina, Father Pennington explained, is "a Christian way to transformation." Jesus summed up the "way" in the two great commandments, then modified the second with the "new" commandment to "love one another as I have loved you." The Benedictine method is summed up in the simple word *lectio* or *lectio divina*, which entails a four-step process: *lectio*, *meditatio*, *oratio*, and *contemplatio*. In Father Pennington's experience, these entail far more than the words suggest in literal translation. In his elaboration of each, we can see how they would lead to transformation, for they aim at nothing less than exposure to the divine Lover.

"*Lectio* most properly resides in hearing [not just reading] the word of God," he says. This may occur not only through Scripture reading but through sermons, music, icons, nature, and other media. The most common form of *lectio* will entail sitting with the Bible in hand, but it may also "mean looking at a work of art, standing before an icon, listening to a friend's word of faith, or taking a walk, letting the beauty of the creation, that often lies beneath layers of sin's ugliness, speak to us." Basil outlined three simple steps that he followed: (1) Come into the presence of God indwelling in the Scriptures and call upon the Spirit to help in hearing. (2) Listen for ten or fifteen minutes. (3) Take a word, a sentence, or a phrase, and thank God. Some days the Scriptures will speak clearly, at other times not so distinctly, and at still others, not at all.

The object of *lectio divina* is to have the mind in us that was also in Christ (Phil. 2:5; 1 Cor. 2:16). This necessitates the other three steps. *Meditatio* involves repeating the word you have received from *lectio*, whether with the lips or in the mind, until it "formed the heart; until, as the [Desert] Fathers sometimes expressed it, the mind descended into the heart." The result of this is *oratio*. *Oratio* means more than our English word "prayer." The desert monks thought of it as "something very powerful and urgent: fiery prayer, darts of fire that shoot out from the heart into the very heart of God. . . . It is prayer in the Holy Spirit. . . . This is pure prayer. For a moment it takes us beyond ourselves. . . . It is a moment when we fulfill the first and greatest commandment: We love the Lord our God with our whole mind, our whole heart, our whole soul, and all our strength." Persons who experience such moments want them to go on and on. This is *contemplatio*, where "the word has so formed us and called us forth, that we abide in total response. Our whole being is a yes to God as he has revealed himself to us. We are, as the Book of Revelation says of Christ, an Amen to the Father."

Father Pennington goes on to remind us that we cannot effect this transformation of consciousness by ourselves. We can prepare ourselves for it by letting go of things that keep us from saying yes to God, that is, we can die to self. "We seek this transformation by listening to the Word of God with openness, letting it in and letting it reform us, through *lectio* and *meditatio*. We can dispose ourselves for transformation by making spaces for God to come in and reveal himself in himself, and in that revealing, transform us."

Here is where Centering Prayer, which occupied such a central place in Basil Pennington's life and ministry, plays a role. Before looking at what it may have contributed to shaping Basil Pennington in the mold of a lover, I pause to take note of one classic of the Hebrew Bible that almost certainly exerted the deepest influence of any on Benedictine and particularly Cistercian spirituality: the Song of Songs. Christian use of it to interpret the covenant between God and the Church and God and the individual soul, dating from Origen's Commentary on the Song of Songs, harked back to Jewish rabbinic interpretation and application. Application of the Song of Songs to a love tryst between God and the individual soul, Ann Matter has observed, "came into its own in the twelfth century," notably in the sermons and commentaries of Bernard of Clairvaux and other Cistercians. Not even St. Benedict himself stood higher and exerted greater influence in Cistercian spirituality than St. Bernard, and none surpassed Bernard in placing love at the very heart and center and in making it the goal of Cistercian spiritual life. Indicative of the impact of this perspective on his own outlook, Father Pennington produced a fresh translation and "spiritual commentary" on the Song of Songs a short time before he died, with illustrations of the text by Jewish artist Phillip Ratner.

Two problems arise here. First, interpretation and application of the Song of Songs in this way erects a high hurdle for a reader trained in modern historical-critical methodology to leap over. The Song of Songs is, on the face of it, a graphic poem describing a love tryst between newlyweds. Will not application in ways that go beyond the love tryst lead to distortion? Father Pennington invokes the history of Christian interpretation to give a resounding no. Because they could not apply all Scriptures literally, the church fathers came up with varied methods to find meaning in all: literal, allegorical or spiritual, moral, and anagogical or unitive. Through the centuries, interpreters have ascribed a *sensus plenior* ("fuller sense") to the Song of Songs as both Jews and Christians viewed it as an analogy for God's love for the chosen people and God's love for the individual. Christians, of course, have often identified the Lover as Christ.

Second, many men find it difficult to relate to the imagery of the Song of Songs because the beloved is a woman. Conscious of their own sex drive, they can't image themselves as brides, as in the Song of Songs. Father Pennington perceived that such feminine imagery accounted for the fact that far more women than men attended Centering Prayer sessions and most church activities. As an alternative, he suggested the image of "friends" that Jesus set forth in John 15:15. Men, too, develop intimate friendships, for instance, in college years, which may last a lifetime. For men, the attractiveness of a friendship with Jesus might well be defeated by some effeminate imaging of Jesus, he thought, judging that such imaging is hardly compatible with the reality.

Such problems as these may prompt you to ask how Basil Pennington could continue to defend the custom of giving persistent and frequent attention to the Song of Songs that Bernard of Clairvaux had made so vital to this tradition. Any answer will surely be complex, but I think it would ultimately boil down to the impact this imagery had on his own formation. Bride and bridegroom by no means supplied the only images that helped him.

In a small volume on monastic practice entitled *Light from the Cloister*, for instance, he devoted a chapter to spiritual friendship and another to Marian devotion. About the latter, he said, "I have known Mary as my Mother since I first came to know her at my mother's knee. My earthly mother, now in heaven, told me my heavenly Mother was a source of love and care. Grandma taught me the rosary at an early age."

Nevertheless, if we want to discover the height and depth, the length and breadth of the love that suffused Basil Pennington's life, we must give full credit to the place of the Song of Songs' imagery in his life. For such a person, a "spiritual commentary" on the Song of Songs, coming so near the end of his life, is a fitting testament of devotion. Like his great forbearer, Bernard of Clairvaux, whom he called "the primary master of the Cistercian school of spirituality" and to whom he introduced many others, he was convinced that God, who is Love, is at the center of our being. And our soul's sincerest desire must be to know God in the most intimate way we can, by love, which is the Spirit of God in us. The Song of Songs figured prominently in the shaping of his understanding of Centering Prayer. He devoted an entire chapter of his classic on Centering Prayer to a meditation based on the fourth poem (2:5–7).

This would seem to be the appropriate place to return to a consideration of the prayer form that held the spotlight in the last quarter century of Basil Pennington's life and that carved a much deserved and permanent niche for him in Cistercian and Christian history. He did not lay claim to anything new. Quite to the contrary, he sought only to "renew" an ancient Christian form of prayer, the Prayer of the Heart or the Jesus Prayer, thus linking Christians of past and present, East and West again. The amount of energy he put into this endeavor surely confirms that Father Pennington found in this form what the saints had sought so earnestly through the centuries, that is, an experience of the loving presence of God. The sale of more than two million copies of *Centering Prayer* shows that many others have felt a pull toward the truth of what he taught.

As Father Pennington was to remind us many times, Centering Prayer is "a very simple method—a technique, if you like that term—to get in touch with what is. . . . It is meant to open the way to living constantly out of the center, to living out of the fullness of who we are." God made us to be God's intimate friends, as Scriptures constantly remind us. "All are called to the intimacy of contemplative union with God, not just a chosen few." Indeed, we are not only called to intimacy "but to take possession of our very oneness with the Son of God in the inner life of the Trinity in the communication of the very Love of the Father and Son, the Most Holy Spirit. This is what Centering Prayer is all about."

His book *Centering Prayer* makes very clear that Father Pennington was not simply engaging in an academic exercise of some kind. He had discovered something of immense significance for his own life that carried with it a commission to share not only with his brothers in the monastery or with Catholic religious but with anyone anywhere seeking meaning and happiness in life. Characteristically, he threw that almost unlimited energy and enthusiasm that he brought to everything he did into the spreading of this simple technique for fulfilling the two great commandments. In doing this, he was in his own very practical way taking a further step beyond the giant step that Thomas Merton had taken in the 1950s and 1960s. This is not the place to discuss Merton's rethinking of monastic *contemptus mundi*, but it is important to note that Merton radically reinterpreted monastic withdrawal and insisted that people "in the world" could benefit from the insight that comes from contemplation. In an essay on "Contemplation in a World of Action," he asserted that "he who attempts to act and do things for others or for the world without deepening his own self-understanding, freedom, integrity, and capacity to love will not have anything to give others. He will communicate to them nothing but the contagion of his own obsessions, his aggressiveness, his ego-centered ambitions, his delusions about ends and means, his doctrinaire prejudices and ideas. . . . Far from being irrelevant, prayer, meditation, and contemplation are of the utmost importance in America today."

What does contemplation offer for someone not living in a monastery? In the strictest sense, the contemplative life is led in monasteries. But in a broader sense, every life can be dedicated to some extent to contemplation, and even the most active of lives can and should be balanced by a contemplative element— leavened by the peace and order and clarity that can be provided by meditation, interior prayer, and the deep penetration of the most fundamental truths of human existence.

In *Thomas Merton, Brother Monk: The Quest for True Freedom*, one of the most insightful studies of Merton's monastic career, Basil Pennington listed Centering Prayer as one of Merton's particular contributions, especially "his insistence that the contemplative experience both as a way of praying and as a dimension of life was meant for all." He quoted an address Merton gave to the community at Gethsemani on the Sunday before Christmas 1965: "I have not only repeated the affirmation that contemplation is real, but I have insisted on its simplicity, sobriety, humility, and its integration in normal Christian life. This is what needs to be stressed. . . . It is surely legitimate for anyone to desire and to seek this fulfillment, this experience of reality, this entrance into truth."

In response to the Merton challenge, Father Pennington wrapped the gift from the desert in a new package and displayed it far and wide. He was like the ancient apostles charged by Jesus to be witnesses in Jerusalem, all of Judaea and Samaria, and to the ends of the earth. *Centering Prayer* even included one chapter entitled "Spreading the Good News" that laid out suggestions for conducting centering groups. "To share Centering Prayer with others is a preeminent way to fulfill our Christian mission, and to open out to our brothers and sisters the Way, the Truth, and the Life; that is, the Good News." In an epilogue, he stated his dream, a dream of a world in which all have discovered the contemplative way:

> I see all the earth in peace, the whole human family living together, sharing the fruits of creation and the joy that comes from the good things of our planet and beyond. And this peace and joy, a universal compassion, flows within and out of the worldwide Christian family. Our brothers and sisters of other faiths, all people of good will, exclaim: "Blessed are the peacemakers, for they are the children of God." And each one of us Christians does indeed know, by personal experience, that he or she is a much-loved child of God. Our lives are filled with love and security, joy and peace. Each one is in touch with his or her own contemplative dimension. Busy days flow out of a deep center. Space is found, time set apart, to enjoy a Father's intimate loving presence and to let him enjoy us.

There will be those who respond by saying, "C'mon, Basil. Snap out of it. Get real. Look at what our world is really like." I must confess that at times I have asked whether dreams like this are illusions conjured up to escape reality. Even now as I write, staggering body counts from Iraq, Somalia torn by Muslim factions, the Holy Land a tinderbox, scores of deaths in Rio de Janeiro in gang fights, New Orleans still devastated from hurricanes, pain beyond pain. In seventy-five years of life (I was born on July 27, 1931, one day before Basil), however, I have found myself coming out again and again on the side of dreamers like this much loved monk.

Dreamers may be more realists than their opposites, for human beings, I am convinced, cannot live without a dream, a vision, of what can be, must be, and will be. Basil's dream was rooted in an experience of what Douglas Steere called "that love which is at the heart of things." And he enabled thousands and thousands of others to get in touch with that reality not only through his teaching of Centering Prayer, but even more, through his buoyant, grace-filled, and radiant personality. May his dream live on.

How Basil Pennington
Came to Kalamazoo

John Sommerfeldt

In 1969, I received an invitation from a hitherto unknown monk, Basil Pennington, to attend a meeting of Cistercian scholars at St. Joseph's Abbey. To fly from Kalamazoo, Michigan, to Spencer, Massachusetts, in those days required time and patience, but more than twenty of us gathered at the monastery.

In addition to prayer and meditation, our days were filled with each scholar's description of his work and plans. I gave a presentation on my plans—very imperfectly realized—to write a multivolume intellectual history of the early Cistercian order. In return, Basil explained to all of us his plans to translate the Cistercian Fathers into English in response to the call of Vatican II to return to the sources of the order's spirituality.

I was deeply impressed with Basil's project and with the response of the Cistercian scholars in attendance. I invited everyone there to attend the next—the sixth—Conference on Medieval Studies sponsored by the Medieval Institute at Western Michigan University and promised to sponsor a Cistercian Conference within the Institute's Conference.

My invitation was accepted and 1971 saw the descent of the Cistercians on Kalamazoo. Basil chaired one of the Cistercian sessions, I the other. Delivering papers were Louis Lekai and Bede Lackner, both distinguished Cistercian historians from Our Lady of Dallas Abbey. Roger DeGanck left his hermitage/trailer at Redwoods to speak to us. Bernie McGinn and Elizabeth Kennan delivered papers. The response of the Cistercians who came was astonishment at the number of scholars who flocked to hear about Bernard and William, about Aelred and Alan of Lille.

Cistercian scholarship found a place within what is now called the International Congress on Medieval Studies and the number of papers and attendees has grown greatly since. By 1976, there were six sessions of Cistercian papers. Among those on the program were Edward McCorkell, Keith Egan, Chrysogonus Waddell, William Pausell, Laurence Braceland, David Bell, and Meredith Lillich.

By this time Basil had experienced firsthand that editing, publishing, and distributing Cistercian translations and studies was more than a one-man job. He approached me with what I thought was a great idea. Basil and I agreed to set up an Institute of Cistercian Studies at Western Michigan University, which would house Cistercian Publications, a Cistercian Library, and arrange the annual Cistercian Conference.

The Abbey of Gethsemani donated its precious Obrecht Collection of manuscripts and incunabula to the library as a permanent loan. And several Cistercian houses served as hosts to meetings of Cistercian scholars, enabling them to experience the life of the order they studied. Although I would oversee the operation of Cistercian Publications as president, Basil and I agreed to hire as editorial director a splendid young scholar Rozanne Elder who had done her master's degree with me and had received her doctorate from the University of Toronto.

For me and my family, the highlight of the move of Cistercian Publications to Kalamazoo was the frequent visits to our home by Basil and other Cistercians—nuns, monks, abbots, even an abbot general—in conjunction with the Cistercian Conference. After the business at the Institute's offices, the group would assemble at the Sommerfeldt house for Mass and one of my wife's, Pat's, splendid meals of many courses. Louis Lekai, Patrick Hart, Chrysogonus Waddell, and Jean Leclerq were always there. Aiden Carr, Sister Gertrude Ballew, and others were less frequent guests because they served on the board for shorter periods.

Basil was, of course, always there. He often came early, which was a source of much delight for our children, Ann, Jim, John, and Elizabeth, who adored him. They lovingly brought him enormous serving bowls filled to overflowing with ice cream. They stood in awe around Basil, watching with delight as he stood on his head. One time, Basil was met at our front door by Jim, then a very skinny high school sophomore. Basil asked Jim what was new in his life. Jim answered that he was now on the wrestling team. Basil then challenged Jim to show him a move, whereupon Jim picked up Basil and deposited that very large man on the living room floor.

Basil rarely spent more than a day at the Conference. He was too busy traveling about visiting charismatic communities in the upper Midwest, especially at the Universities of Michigan and Notre Dame. Each day, he would teach meditative techniques and celebrate numerous liturgies. Despite his degree in canon law, Basil rarely observed the canons—the liturgical ones at least. He once told me that in pre-Vatican II days, canon law had dictated moral theology. After Vatican II, Basil was delighted to observe, moral theology, the law of love, superseded the institutional rules and regulations of canon law.

Basil's enthusiasm for meditation and his generosity in sharing his rich experience with meditative techniques led my wife, Pat, and me to participate in a week-long seminar with this master meditator. The group was composed mostly of Cistercian monks—with a Discalced Carmelite nun as a welcome guest. After several sessions of instruction, it came time to try our wings—or, rather, allow the Spirit to open us up to reality. I had just finished entertaining some four thousand of my nearest and dearest friends at the International Medieval Congress, and I was exhausted. Meditative relaxation soon led to deep sleep and a rude awakening from wifely pokes in the ribs. "You were snoring," Pat admonished indignantly. Father Felix, then from Gethesemani Abbey, commented dryly: "Oh, I thought that was his mantra." Basil was blissfully unaware of this byplay. Indeed, one of the most endearing qualities of the man was his seemingly constant state of bliss.

When news of Basil's terrible, final trauma came, I was horrified not only by the event but by its cause in an automobile accident. My experience with Basil's driving was uniformly terrifying. Once, when Basil was driving me from New Melleray to Mississippi Abbey, we crossed the rolling Iowa countryside on a narrow gravel road. Basil was doing at least seventy as we approached an unmarked crossroad at the same time as a huge dump truck. The truck driver only narrowly missed destroying us. It took me a good while to calm down. Basil, on the other hand, remained blissfully unaware of the existence of the crossroad or the massive truck.

Some time later—it was 1973, as I remember—Basil and I crisscrossed monastic Belgium and the Netherlands on our way to the Anglican-Cistercian-Orthodox Conference at Oxford, England. Basil was folded up in the Volkswagen Beetle I had rented, and several times he volunteered to share the driving chore. I steadfastly refused, citing my need to hold onto the steering wheel to brace my bad back. This was true, but it was not the whole truth.

Basil's inability to recognize danger was but one evidence of his complete trust and total absorption in the love of God. He was—and is—a truly holy man. I miss him, and I look forward to our joyous reunion.

List of Papers Given at the Inaugural Cistercian
Studies Conference in Kalamazoo

1971

Cistercian Studies I
Monday, May 12, 1971
1:30 PM
Chairman: M. Basil Pennington, OCSO, St. Joseph's Abbey

"The Ideological Roots of Early Cîteaux."
Bede Lackner [O. Cist.], University of Texas, Arlington

"The Abbot of Cîteaux:
His Name, Place, and Jurisdiction in the Cistercian Order."
Roger De Ganck [O. Cist.], Redwoods Abbey

"Abbot Martin of Pairis and the Fourth Crusade."
Alfred J. Andrea, The University of Vermont

"The Frontier of Spanish Reconquest and the Landed
Acquisitions of the Cistercians of Poblet, 1150–1276."
Lawrence McCrank, The University of Virginia

"The College of St. Bernard in Toulouse."
Louis J. Lekai [O. Cist.], University of Dallas

Cistercian Studies II
Tuesday, May 13, 1971
1:30 PM
Chairman: John R. Sommerfeldt, Western Michigan University

"St. Bernard's *De consideration*: Contradiction and Politics."
Elizabeth T. Kennan, The Catholic University of America

"William of St.-Thierry against Peter Abelard:
A Dispute on the Meaning of Being a Person."
Thomas M. Tomasic, John Carroll University

"Eschatology in the Advent Sermons of Aelred of Rievaulx."
Linda Spear, Pontifical Institute of Mediaeval Studies

"The Significance of the Cistercian Treatises on the Soul."
Bernard McGinn, The University of Chicago

"The Monastic Vocation of Alan of Lille."
John Trout, Hanover College

REFLECTION

Werner Erhard

Basil Pennington was a light in my life, just as he was in many people's lives. There was a profound spiritual space around Basil that was large enough and tangible enough that everyone could experience it and be part of it. When he led a program, his face was a clear expression of inner joy that made what he had to offer very available to people. Basil had a very easy way about him. He could say things that were penetrating, but say them in a way that people were open to and could hear. And—even though Basil was a deeply committed and religious man—he himself was open to exploring and finding value in nontraditional ideas that might not immediately look compatible with his calling.

Basel's commitment to be of service to others was evident in the way he made himself available. There is a famous allegory in Zen Buddhism called the ten ox-herding pictures. The pictures and the accompanying story illustrate the journey of the individual on the path to enlightenment, to discovering the true self. Originally, there were only eight ox-herding pictures, and the eighth picture, the one that represented achieving what Basil might have called spiritual enlightenment, was an empty circle. Later, one of the Zen patriarchs added two pictures to the original eight. Now in the last picture, the person who has achieved his own enlightenment has returned to the world to minister to those still on the journey. That picture is the perfect expression of who Basil was for me.

A Life Lived Abundantly

Ann Overton

The first time I was with Basil Pennington, I peeked. A group of us were meeting to discuss what would later become the Mastery Foundation, and we had stopped for lunch. In the midst of the noonday bustle of the restaurant, Basil invited us to bow our heads as he said a blessing before our meal.

Listening to his words, I began to think someone else had sat down at the table with us. This prayer was not addressed to some remote deity; Basil was talking to a friend who had just pulled up a chair. The feeling was so real, I couldn't help myself. I lifted up my head and peeked. But it was only our original group at the table—along with the invisible but unmistakable presence Basil had invoked to join and bless us.

Over the next twenty-five years, I was to witness how present God was for Basil. God was not an idea, an encounter, or even a memory of an encounter. God was an abundant, living presence, as real to Basil as any of us at the table that day.

That Basil and I met at all was partly due to his frustration that the presence of God was not equally available to all who were called to religious ministry. Throughout his own ministry, he was committed to having everyone who ministered discover the contemplative dimension in their own lives and be freed to make the difference they were called to make. He described this intention as "waking the sleeping giants" and liberating the enormous energy and potential in churches, synagogues, and the entire network of religious institutions.

So in the early 1980s, a handful of like-minded individuals began the conversations that would result in the creation of the Mastery Foundation in 1983. We found each other through our experience of a personal development program called The est Training. Sometime in the late 1970s, a friend had told Basil about The est Training and its creator, Werner Erhard. From the beginning, est was both immensely popular and controversial. (Some said it was part of the New Age movement of spirituality; Basil always said the New Age began with the birth of Christ.)

While I never knew Basil's religious and doctrinal beliefs to stray from the teachings of the Roman Catholic Church, he was remarkably open to new experiences. In fact, he was very suspicious of decisions and insight based on theory alone. He believed that you judge a tree by its fruit. Knowledge gained and tested through your own experience was far richer and more trustworthy than knowledge acquired by hearsay. His axiom, which we practice to this day, was "experience first, discuss later."

So where others belittled or dismissed the experience of personal transformation available in The est Training, Basil found tools that could be used by women and men of faith to continually renew the power of their ministries and their ability to make a positive, lasting difference. In February 1984, Basil and Werner delivered the Mastery Foundation's first program, "Making a Difference: A Course for Those Who Minister."

Over the next two decades, those of us privileged to know Basil through the Mastery Foundation would continue to experience and benefit from the abundance of life, love, and possibility he brought into our lives.

Maybe it helped that he looked like he had been sent over from central casting to play Santa Claus. He was a big bear of a man, given to hugs that matched his size and his enthusiasm for meeting friends, old and new. He was simply and fully who and what he was in a way that made you feel you could be fully who you were, too.

There was just such an extravagant abundance about him. As a young Catholic, Basil would have been instructed in the doctrine of the church through the Baltimore Catechism. But when I think of Basil, I think of the older (and Protestant) Westminster Shorter Catechism and its more effusive language: "What is the chief end of man?" The answer, which was also Basil's answer, is, "Man's chief end is to glorify God, and enjoy him forever."

One summer, he and I were invited to a large family picnic— though I suspect I was there as someone who knew what to do with a monk at a picnic. Basil was in the swimming pool when I arrived, tossing a beach ball with a group of children. As he dried himself off, I told him I found it odd that his suntan was better than mine. "Oh," he said, "I've been giving a retreat and during the afternoon break, I enjoy lying in the sun. You know, one must enjoy all of God's gifts."

That was Basil, a man who truly enjoyed the abundance of God's gifts. As a Trappist, the Cistercians who follow the strictest rule of community life, his diet at the monastery was vegetarian. When he was traveling, however, he could and did eat whatever he wanted. He had interesting stories about food, because his practice and delight in restaurants was to order anything on the menu he had never eaten before. He also usually ordered and ate two desserts.

He was equally bold in his ministry and often reminded me of a statement attributed to Sigmund Freud, "How bold one is when one is sure of being loved."

Once when we were meeting in early January, he suggested to me that the Mastery Foundation buy space in the *National Catholic Reporter* newspaper advertising a "Making a Difference" course we were having during Lent. Here is what he thought the ad should say:

> Is your priest dead?
> Send him to us.
> We will resurrect him
> in time for Easter.

He was serious. I'm sorry to say now that I was not bold enough to do it.

There wasn't anything particularly "holy" about Basil to me, or I think to any of us who worked closely with him. He certainly didn't come across as someone who thought himself important. He knew hundreds of individuals, many of them intimately, and yet I never heard him speak of anyone except in the most glowing terms. Nor did he come across as someone overly devout or humble. What really struck you about him was just how incredibly alive and full of joy he was.

I asked him once if he ever battled doubt, despair, or depression. He looked surprised for a moment at the question, then quietly smiled at me and said, "No." I have to think he was being honest with me, because in all the time I knew him, only once was I with him when he seemed preoccupied and slightly removed.

Being a priest and a monk was his calling, his commitment, his work, his labor of love. For all his enjoyment of the secular world, he was a man of prayer who relished silence as much as that second dessert. I sometimes joke that one way to end a gathering quickly is to say, "Let us pray." But when Basil said it, you were drawn into an experience of peace and contemplation.

In fact, the Mastery Foundation and the "Making a Difference" workshop were formed out of deep concern not only for those who minister but for the world as a whole. Basil considered it almost tragic that ministries and religions did not have more impact on bringing peace and a sense of community to the modern world, and he could be very bold in how he spoke about it.

Three years before he died, he said, "Corporate executives have said to me, 'If I had the manpower and the money the Catholic Church has and as little effect, I'd close down tomorrow.' We're not at all making the difference we could be making. Most clergy realize that, and it's very frustrating and depressing."

But as frustrated as he sometimes felt, he never wavered in seeing the abundance of possibilities ministers of all faiths could bring to those they serve. In an interview we taped in 1995, he said:

> What is ministry but bringing people the Good News? And now you don't bring the Good News as something you read and studied and picked up in seminary. But it's something that's alive in you. You are the good news, and you bring this to people. And you really communicate because you're wide open to their space, and they're open to your space then. It really transforms ministry. It isn't the sort of thing you get down to mathematical formulas like two and two equals four. It's an experience, the experience of life and love and transformation and resurrection. And we're seeing it happen all the time in our Making a Difference graduates.
>
> Here we are reaching out to all, to enliven the whole spiritual movement. The place religions get into trouble when we try to talk to each other from different traditions is that we have a whole background that expresses our experience in certain words, certain concepts. Some of them have been bought and developed at great price, through centuries of struggle. It's been my experience in meditation, when we go to that deeper level and are together in the silence, we experience a real communion.

We realize that something else has happened there. But our conceptual stuff is so limited.

The whole call of the Vatican Council was ecumenical and interreligious union, communion, and affirmation, working together for the well-being of all. This is the only place where I've really seen that all coming together.

Perhaps it was the influence of his friend and fellow Cistercian Thomas Merton. Or perhaps it was, once again, that innate context of abundance and possibility Basil brought to everything. But long before interfaith work was considered important, Basil saw the need to support and empower all those whose lives are about sacred ministry, and to do it in a way that was neither superficial or fanatical. To him, life and ministry were rich, abundant gifts to be savored, enjoyed, and shared with all.

No one who knew him could miss his ability to awaken the possibilities and passion that lay dormant in others. He did this so well that I came to refer to him as the Trappist's turnaround man. Three times, his order sent him to breathe new life into struggling communities. At one monastery, he started a successful fruitcake business. (Part of one of our board meetings that year was given over to tasting fruitcakes made from different recipes.) His wealthier friends would greet each new assignment warily, knowing they would soon be hearing about a campaign for capital improvements. And always, in a church where religious orders have fewer and fewer new members, he would recruit a new class of young men to a life of prayer and devotion.

He made it seem effortless. Indeed, he would have made a great corporate chief executive officer—a trait I didn't always appreciate when as chairman of our all-volunteer board he assumed there would always be someone else to carry out every task. Once in awhile, someone would question his almost universal use of male pronouns in referring to God. He had grown up and been shaped by an era of male domination and hierarchy both inside and outside the Church, but he always graciously rethought this behavior when it was pointed out to him.

After the first few years of working with Basil and the other men and women of faith I met through the Mastery Foundation, it struck me one day that I was often in the presence of living saints. After all, those who knew St. Francis or St. Catherine surely knew them as remarkable humans, but their designation as saints came much later. So don't we also have the privilege of knowing saints in our midst? I'm sure if Basil were alive, he would be able to name them in abundance.

Abundance. I will always think of that as his gift to us. As he said,

> You don't have to carry everything on your shoulders all the time. That's a great breakthrough for some people. This new vitalization within you. A sense of how much you're loved and how precious a person you are and that you can really make a difference—you yourself, not what you do, not what you have, not what other people think of you, but you.
>
> You are presence and can bring life, and love, and vitality to people. The tremendous freeing, the empowerment, the fullness, the source of being and life in us is able finally to be there as gift and life and hope to everybody. You reflect back to people then in a very pure way their own beauty, their own wonder, and you get them in touch with how much God really loves them.
>
> So it's a very, very powerful thing in our lives. It really transforms us, you know. It enables us to transform the space of ministry, where everything is possible. And wonderful

things happen because there is real communication and love. That is a world that really begins to be something that God designed it to be—a community of people who are caring, sharing, and using the enormous potential of the earth for the well-being of the whole human family.

Part Five

HUMAN BEING AND FRIEND

Welcoming the Stranger

Arnold Mark Belzer

As Abraham sat at the door of his tent one day at about noon, he saw three men approaching. He ran to meet them, bowed down before them, and invited them to rest in his tent and partake of some refreshment. Calling Sarah, his wife, he told her to make some cakes of the finest flour. He caused the best calf of his herds to be killed to feed the unknown visitors. Butter, milk and honey were also placed before them, Abraham himself waiting upon his guests. After the meal, when they were about to depart, one of the strangers said to Abraham that after a year he would return, and that Sarah, his wife, would have a son. Then Abraham understood that the Lord God Himself, accompanied by angels, was his guest. Kindness and courtesy to strangers should be praised and encouraged, since God rewarded so richly the hospitality of Abraham. (Gen. 18:2–10)

As Christians have Christmas and Easter, Jews have their equivalents; standing room only is expected on Rosh Hashanah (the Jewish New Year) and Yom Kippur (the Day of Atonement). But a standing-room only crowd at my synagogue, Congregation Mickve (the hope of) Israel in Savannah, Georgia, was quite a surprise on the ordinary weekday night of February 12, 1992. It wasn't a Jewish holiday; it was Georgia Day, the commemoration of the founding of the State of Georgia in 1733.

It has been the tradition of the Historic Houses of Worship Association of Savannah to hold an interfaith service to honor Georgia's anniversary. Since the chairman of the Mastery Foundation, Father Basil Pennington, was to be in Savannah for a board meeting and since my congregation was to be the host for the Georgia Day Interfaith service, it seemed entirely fitting that Basil give the sermon for the service. Thus the synagogue was packed at Mickve Israel on that February evening!

As I scanned the crowd, it seemed different. I could easily recognize my own members as well as many of the members of the mainline Protestant congregations in our historic district. I also knew many of the members of the Catholic cathedral, but other folks were present, folks I hadn't counted on to be there. As it turned out, they were Catholics from some of the surrounding Catholic parishes and others from the surrounding country towns. They had come to hear Father Basil.

Though I had known Basil since 1980, we had shared our experiences with Mastery in relatively small groups of sixty to one hundred. I had never experienced him in a large group of several hundred. Now, in my synagogue sanctuary I experienced a most gifted and inspired pastor who welcomed hundreds of people of diverse religious orientations into his spiritual realm. His words moved the worshipers, but more important, he invited those present not only into a world as close as their hearts and minds but also into a world that many had not known existed. It was then that I realized how natural his presence was in the beautiful Gothic sanctuary of our historic congregation, and how much he brought to mind the hospitality of my ancestors Abraham and Sarah.

Because of the combination of both Jewish and Southern tradition, our congregation has always been devoted to the practice of hospitality, considering it a "double commandment." Now in the spirit of commanded hospitality, Basil Pennington stood in the pulpit of the only gothic synagogue in America and by his formidable presence and well-chosen words managed to invite an entire congregation into his world, a world where one could encounter the presence in moments of quiet contemplation.

The extraordinary standard of hospitality Basil exemplified was evident at the very first workshop of the Mastery Foundation in 1984. I will never ever forget the many volunteers who warmly greeted new arrivals to the conference center and carried luggage to their rooms. Even more impressive were the little pink squares of paper printed with little check-offs for: water, coffee, tea, or soft drink. Participants needed only to check-off their needs, hold up the little pink square of paper, and a volunteer, almost unseen snatched it and within only a few moments a cup of coffee (or whatever) appeared almost as if it was magic. What a model of hospitality!

I also experienced Basil's hospitality at St. Joseph's Abbey in Spencer, Massachusetts, in one of the most memorable encounters of my life. At the very end of October, I was in the area to pick up a custom-made door for a new home I was building. I had never visited a monastery before, but I felt that I had to visit Basil in the environment he so loved. I arrived after dinner, and Basil welcomed me in his very special, blessed way. He took me to my quarters, a beautiful stone guesthouse. Basil asked me if I would like to attend the early morning Office. I am definitely not an early morning person, but I was anxious to see the monastery in the daylight. I rose in that very early light and went off to an imposing chapel. As I walked the grounds, I wondered: was the monastery built so impeccably and beautifully just to attract novices?

Basil met me with good morning greetings; again I felt incredibly welcomed. During the service, the voices of the monks were spectacular. It seemed to me that they must have auditioned to be accepted into the order. The liturgy was quite inspiring. The homily was excellent. I was somewhat surprised to hear a message that noted the close proximity that year of the Jewish holiday of Simchat Torah (Rejoicing of the Law) and All Saints Day.

Father Basil's hospitality included providing me with a unique, talented, and very blessed breakfast companion—the monk who gave the homily, Father Bernard. We ate our breakfast in a private dining room and continued our discussion until almost noon. Whether Father Basil knew about our connection or not, I do not know. I never asked him, instead relishing the miracle of propinquity, as Father Bernard and I quickly came to realize that we both had been "Bar Mitzvahed" at the age of thirteen by the same rabbi! It is a long story, so suffice it to say that Father Bernard and I had come from similar backgrounds and experiences, and yet here we were in a Trappist monastery in the hills of Massachusetts—a rabbi and a monk! We could just as well have been each other—he the rabbi and I the monk. And we were brought together by a "monk's monk" and a "rabbi's monk," Basil Pennington.

Father Basil, like our father Abraham, welcomed the stranger with warm hospitality inviting me into his spiritual world, his spiritual home, and his fellowship of brothers and colleagues. As we say in our Jewish tradition: may his memory be for us a blessing.

Lessons in Love

Franck Perrier

How did a twenty-three-year-old French student meet Basil Pennington? In July 1984, I left home for the Charles de Gaulle airport, outside of Paris. I was about to spend two semesters at Northeastern University in Boston obtaining my bachelor's degree in business administration. This was not a two-week trip. I had tidied up my room, said good-bye to my mother, partied with my friends. There was nothing left in Paris for me for the next ten months. I was eager and a little anxious to live that American experience. Once I arrived at the airport, it was announced that my low-cost flight was delayed for twelve hours. I decided to go back home rather than wait in the airport. So I found myself back in my room, a little depressed—I remember that moment as if it were yesterday—sitting on my bed, with nothing to do, no one I wanted to call.

A few weeks before leaving, I had asked my parents if they had any connections in the U.S. After all, I was about to spend a year in Boston and I knew absolutely no one there. My father, who is a profound atheist but sensitive to monastic environments, said he would talk to Dom Eugene Manning, the superior of the Cistercian community in eastern France. He had previously given me the name of Father Basil Pennington, whom I had written, but since I had never received an answer, I had not given it much thought.

Now, here I was back home in Paris waiting for my flight to America, and the idea just popped up in my head that I would call this Basil Pennington. I expected nothing, really. I was not sure I could reach him and had no plans in mind. But there he was on the phone. I explained who I was. "Did you receive my letter?" "No, I do not recall receiving a letter from you." "I am a French student, coming from Paris, France, for a year in Boston. I got your name from Superior Dom Eugene Manning who is a good friend of my father. I will land at Logan Airport at 6 AM on Sunday." "Well, I have a flight at 8 AM. Why don't you wait for me at the airport?" "Fine. How will I recognize you?" "Oh you will."

I met Basil at the airport around 6:30 AM. He is a man one can't miss. He had arranged for me to stay at a convent in downtown Boston for a week, until I could find accommodations on my own. He helped me start my life in the U.S. and would support me regularly over the next few months. We would see each other often until I moved to San Francisco in 1987. We also wrote each other often until 1990. He has been with me since that Sunday of July 1985, and he will be with me until my death. His death has not changed anything about his presence in my life, I just regret that I did not take the time to visit him more.

At Spencer where I spent a few days for a retreat, at Nantucket when we visited his friend Paul, in Boston on his way back and forth from Spencer, in Tiburon near San Francisco where I was living in 1987 and 1988, or in Paris after 1998, our meetings would always be about love, about greatness, about making a difference in this world. At the same time, Basil revealed such gigantic humanity. I particularly appreciated how he accepted my results or lack of results. Or rather, how performance and producing results were not an objective. Yet they flew from his being. Remember that as a business student, raised by my education and family to be "the best" and in an environment built around productivity, results were my bread and butter. I felt great relief to see someone operate with other values. For even though Basil was a great networker and achiever, he allowed others—and possibly himself—to fail occasionally.

Basil taught me Centering Prayer, and we could center anywhere, anytime. We would just sit and meditate for twenty minutes. Sometimes I would doze, sometimes he would. I asked him about that, and he said it was fine. A few years later, while visiting in Paris, he celebrated Mass in my small one-bedroom apartment, where I would more often party than share the Eucharist. I was touched by all these simple ways of living his faith. It felt so real, human, and true. It also was disconnected from the dogma of the Catholic Church that to me often seems distant from everyday life. Basil was an extremely sophisticated and complex man who had brought the essential things of life back to their true essence by making them look so simple and authentic.

In another conversation about churches and followers, I happened to mention Reverend Moon of the Unification Church. This organization is strongly opposed in France and perceived as a dangerous sect. Basil said he had met Reverend Moon and that he was a good man. The exact word may not have been "good," but it was respectful enough to strike me that he trusted the strength of his experience over the global rumor.

Basil was a great thinker but also extremely practical. I reproduce here from his own handwritten notes what he called a "rule of life." Here is an easy-to-use method for one's everyday life, at home or in one's professional environment.

1. Goals: short term and long term
2. What do you need to reach these?
3. What has been preventing you from reaching your goals?
4. What is your program: daily—weekly—monthly?

In another discussion, I asked him about happiness, and here is what he answered, "Happiness is knowing what you want and knowing that you have it or that you are on the way of getting it." Whether he quoted someone or not, doesn't that make a lot of sense? It did to me, and I was pretty unhappy at the time.

Basil was a busy man, involved in numerous activities, with significant responsibilities within and outside his community. He did not particularly care about fundraising programs, he said, "But it needs to be done." He was hugely successful at it. His business mind was often at work—how could he create revenue for his community? While he was visiting monasteries in California in 1987, he wrote to me that he had learned about making fruitcakes. He traveled extensively, and I remember his schedule would be well-committed two years in advance. He did have to learn to say "no." Enjoying being back home in the summer of 1986, he wrote me that he was hoping to stay home for the rest of the year "in spite of the fact that since I have returned, I have been invited to India to do a TV show with the Dalai Lama, to Ireland, to Indonesia, and to the Philippines."

He was a prolific and talented writer, and sold millions of copies of his books. In the summer of 1985, he asked me to help on the organization of *Breaking Bread*. He would easily share about his work with his friends in order to sharpen his editorial vision, to try out ideas, to clarify and sharpen his thinking. He was very keen on getting his message of love and "doing justice to the Lord. . . . If what I write cannot make a difference in the reader's life, I don't want to waste time publishing." I humbly helped him in his writing when I could, and when he needed me, translated into French articles on Centering Prayer. I got more involved in the book *Centered Living*. He would send me the chapters one after the other, and I would make suggestions, even corrections, discussing the title of each chapter, giving insights and different angles. I very much enjoyed this working relationship.

Basil enjoyed life in a simple way. In July 1985, I had just graduated from Northeastern University and had filed for a working visa as an accountant for a fashion company in New York. I had a few free weeks ahead of me, and Basil and I took off for the island of Nantucket to visit his friends Paul and Larry. He enjoyed swimming. Quite often in his letters, he would mention that he would get in a swim. In Paris, he enjoyed staying at my mother's apartment, where he was always welcome. He liked his bedroom, which had been mine, and the home cooking.

In a letter dated October 15, 1986, he wrote: "New England is in all her glory now. Today is crystal clear and the hills are a riot of colors. A frost last week got the dahlias, but the marigolds and mums are still adding their bit to the colors. The great oak amazes me. I watch the color come into the top and seep down. What a magnificent sight now."

Basil also introduced me to a number of people who either became dear friends or who made a difference in my business life. In November 1987, he wrote Werner Erhard about me, "I have a young friend—indeed, he is more than a friend, more like a son to me." Now that I am a young father, forty-six years old, and more fully understand what that means, there are no doubts that Basil was a father to me. He inspired and still inspires my life everyday.

A final memory. Soon after my arrival in Boston, there he was, standing in my two-bedroom apartment in Somerville. After the warm welcome and the usual hug, we started to talk as we always would. Somewhere in our conversation, Basil told me I was a beautiful person and that it was fine to be loved for who I was. This time I heard what he said—it sunk in. It moved me so much that I started to cry.

My childhood had been a happy one. I was loved by my grandparents, loved by my mother (even though she never said the words), and loved by my father as much as he could (he was not in the "loving" business).

On September 19, 1987, Basil wrote me: "You know my very special love for you. You are in each day's prayer. I am happy that you are having this new opportunity to grow. I am happy, too, that the meditation is helping you." That message of love seems so simple, almost easy and common. Each of us has his or her personal history and a lover, a mother, a father, a relative, a friend who once gave us a message of love that really touched us. That this man could simply open up and share his love for me, touched me deeply where I had been hurt in my life. That moment would become a foundation in my life, a small rebirth, and Basil would stay with me for the rest of my life.

REFLECTION

Erik P. Goldschmidt

It was a crisp New England autumn Saturday, the first sunny day in weeks. Pulling onto the Massachusetts Turnpike, I was not only leaving Boston but fleeing the stress it represented for me. As a doctoral student in psychology, I was interning at a school for children with severe psychological and behavioral problems while attending evening classes, conducting research with my advisor, and working to make ends meet. Throw in sleep deprivation, and it is no surprise that my life was far from centered. That week had been a particularly difficult one.

The miles flew by at nearly the same rate my mind was racing. *How am I going to get all of this done? Will it be worth all these years of struggle? Did I make the right decision in starting this doctorate?* I remember turning up the radio to distract myself. This was one of several trips I had taken to St. Joseph Abbey to visit Basil. I typically regarded them as retreats, but this visit had more of an air of desperation and seeking to preserve my sanity.

When I arrived, Basil told me he had enjoyed reading my thesis on Merton. Then he took me to his office and, without uttering a word, handed me a clear plastic bag. I chuckled to myself knowing how much Cistercians communicate through their silence. Sealed inside the bag was a postcard addressed to Basil from Thailand. It was a note from Merton dated a week before Merton's tragic death in Bangkok. My own stunned silence was the only appropriate response.

Basil then motioned for me to follow him outside, leading me to an old pickup truck. Minutes later, we were bouncing our way along faint dirt roads through the deep woods of the monastery property. Basil told me he had walked these paths many times in his fifty years as a monk. I shared with Basil my anxiety about all the commitments with which I had entangled my life. I remember his response was a subtle expression of disbelief, a look only a monk could be capable of giving. In that moment, the absurdity of the thin self-importance of my hyperactive life became quite apparent to me.

We pulled onto a rise in a field with a grand view of the countryside. Basil turned and told me how he was attending Twelve Step programs, the support groups created by Alcoholics Anonymous for addicts in recovery. Now I looked at him with disbelief as he explained that even though he was not an alcoholic, attending these groups helped his own prayer life. With each step, group members accept that they are powerless and that only God or a power greater than themselves can restore them to wholeness. Basil then commented on the beauty of the scenery and how many autumns he had enjoyed the foliage from that vantage point. His words drew my attention to the surrounding landscape—a dazzling display of color that my busy thoughts had blinded me from seeing until then. I smiled again.

The stillness that pervaded the monastery and Basil's life stayed with me as I drove home to Boston that night. I recalled a talk Basil had given in New York City several years earlier. He had explained that Centering Prayer involves consenting to God's presence and movement within ourselves, choosing to quiet ourselves, and being willing to give control of our lives over to God. I arrived home with my mind at ease and my sanity restored.

I remember many visits like this with my friend and brother Basil Pennington. His words and presence were sacramental.

Sharing this story about Father Basil brings great joy to me. With gratitude, I conclude with words Basil wrote in his reflection on his brother monk Thomas Merton, in remembrance, "of this wonderful, intensely human man, who really got hold of what it means to be a Christian and a monk . . . who joyfully and fearlessly sought to live to the full without rejecting in any way the fullness of his humanity."

Surrendered to Love
The Challenge of Living Prayer

David G. Benner

The relationship between an author and a reader can seem impersonal, but it has the potential to be remarkably intimate. I first met Father Basil Pennington in the early 1980s through his book *Centering Prayer*. Deeply affected by this book, I began to work backward through his earlier books and at the same time attempted to keep abreast of his new ones. As anyone who has scanned the total list of his written output could easily appreciate, this was quite a challenge.

By reading his books over the years before I met him in person, I was not simply getting to know the information he was imparting. I was, in fact, getting to know him. It may have been a one-way relationship, but it was a real relationship. Relationships with authors can be life changing.

I think of that often when I meet people who, noting that Father Basil wrote endorsements for several of my own books, are eager to tell me stories about how affected they have been by things he has written. One woman told me of having read Father Basil's discussion of the unique blessing of vigils as a night prayer watch. As a married woman with several young children, she was not immediately sure how she could incorporate the blessing that he bore witness to, but she resolved to try. She found a way to wake up at 3:30 AM without disturbing her husband and children, to get dressed and go to a room in her house where she could read a psalm and then sit in silence before her Lord for twenty minutes. Ten years later, she still did this at least once a week, and not only had it become central to her spiritual practice, it was one of the places of her deepest meeting with God.

I first met Father Basil in person when I was at the Monastery of the Holy Spirit in Conyers, Georgia, on a retreat. He was abbot at the time and met with several of us during the retreat. When he discovered I was a psychologist with a primary interest in the interaction of spirit and soul, we talked about books we were both writing and of the possibility of collaborating on some areas of overlapping interest.

Several months later, I got an e-mail from him saying he had left Georgia and had returned to the Abbey of St. Joseph in Spencer, Massachusetts—the monastery he had first entered as a young man on June 18, 1951. He went on to speak of some of the challenges he was facing in his transition into retirement, and he told me how deeply affected he had been by my book, *Surrender to Love*. He had just returned from a week in the Hermitage at St. Joseph, where he had spent his time prayerfully working through this little book. He asked if I would come to the monastery and help him process some of the issues that had surfaced for him as he read it.

I went, and we spent eight to ten hours in intense dialogue for each of the four days I was with him. This was followed by regular e-mail over the next year and a second retreat that took the same form the following year. Once again, regular e-mail contact followed as we prepared for a third retreat. His sudden and tragic death on June 3, 2005, came before I could return.

So while I first met him through his book on Centering Prayer, I came to really know him as a lived expression of a centered life. It is that centered life that most deeply touched me, and I am convinced that it was that centered life that allowed him to touch so many other people.

It is a challenge to move from offering prayers to living prayer—
that is, making one's life a ceaseless prayer whether or not one
is conscious of praying. A life that is truly centered in prayerful
awareness of and openness to God's gracious presence is a life
of lived prayer. Monastic living undoubtedly offers significant
advantages in movement toward such a centered life, but progress
on this journey is no more automatic for monks than it is for the
rest of us.

Father Basil knew both the advantages and the challenges of
living prayer. The deeply internalized rhythms of the monastic
life—particularly the Liturgy of the Hours—had come to be an
anchor for his spirit and soul. Long practice of Centering Prayer
had taught him to quickly enter into God's presence in stillness
and move out from this with a keener sense of that continuing
presence.

His retirement years were short but challenging. Retirement
would probably be a significant adjustment for anyone who had
lived his unique combination of a contemplative and active life
for so long. Quite suddenly, his public life of travel and speaking
ended, and he found himself immersed in the contemplative
stillness that had been his enduring vocation and that he embraced
as God's special gift for this stage of his life. The openness to his
personal depths that accompanied the deeper stillness brought
pangs of regret, of unfinished (and in some cases unfinishable)
business, and of loss intermixed with the ache of old hurts and
fresh disappointments, and these sometimes got in the way of his
ability to remain open in trust and surrender before God.

He spoke with me often about how he handled these inner
sources of distress, always seeking accountability as a check
against dishonesty and against dealing with these issues in
any way that would limit his growth and movement toward
wholeness. He was committed to being open in truth before

himself, God, and his brothers in community, and it was the disciplines and structures of his life that kept him centered and open and provided him with the healing and deep meeting of God that he sought.

Stillness combined with expectant openness and trust was the default position of his life. This was the place to which he returned regardless of what might arise out of the openness. Things can certainly be counted on to arise out of openness in silence and stillness. Often it was messages from his inner depths. These he learned to note but then gently release—returning at a later point for prayerful reflection on them (and sometimes dialogue with others). It was, he once told me, like breathing in—pausing—and then breathing out. Breathing in is receiving whatever comes to consciousness. It must be received. To try and reject it is to choke and gag. But then, after a pause, it must be released. To attempt to hold onto it is like trying to hold one's breath. You can do it for a short time, but eventually the breath must be released. So, too, it is with the things that come to consciousness in stillness.

This basic posture of receiving his experience in openness—without defensiveness, judgment, or a need to fix or change it—was the ground of his life. This kept him centered. Without this openness to self, any apparent openness to God would have been seriously limited. He knew this, and he kept himself grounded by living this prayer of acceptance, openness, and trust.

But a centered life is a life of openness both to self and God. This is where *lectio* entered the picture. By this point in his life, the practice of Centering Prayer and *lectio divina* were seamlessly interwoven. It was the dance of silence and the Word expressed in the rhythm of openness and surrender.

He shared often about his discoveries and insights from *lectio*. Here God spoke through the Scriptures and other readings. Father Basil sought to make all his reading *lectio*—never simply reading for information but rather reading to hear God's voice. Here he consciously worked on the things that floated to the surface in Centering Prayer, the complement to centering that deepened his openness to God and self.

Centering and *lectio* are right at the core of Christian prayer because they involve the opening of one's self in truth and trust to God. Prayer is that two-fold openness to self and God that allows one to commune with God in one's depths. We either bring to prayer our true self or a false, lying self. Father Basil taught me by his life the courage that was involved in bringing one's true self—the courage of meeting God in the midst of present reality, not in some place of pretence.

Vladimir Lossky, whose writings Father Basil introduced me to, speaks powerfully of this openness to self that is essential to being grounded in God. He argues that in prayer "nothing must be held back . . . every opening of self to the essence of Self is appropriate, for seen this way prayer is the motive power behind all human efforts and every presence of man before the face of God is a prayer." This is the prayer that God desires to receive from us—not just lips that say the proper words but the soul that speaks its truth in openness and faith.

Father Basil's contribution to the discovery (or recovery) of these practices in the last several decades has been immense. His books, articles, and workshops have been the vehicles that brought these practices as gifts of God to many of us. He did not merely practice Centering Prayer, he lived it. And he lived *lectio divina*. These became so deeply a part of his life that everything else flowed out of this place of stillness, openness, and attentiveness.

Presence to self and presence to God were the foundation of a life that allowed others to meet God in his life and words. He was far from perfect; nevertheless, he dared to live the truth of his imperfections and the reality of his broken humanness in openness before God. His life was, therefore, prayer. I thank God for the gift that his life was to me and to all those who have encountered him in person or through his writing.

Set Us Free, O God
Basil and Dance

——◆——

Bruce Stewart

There he was, sitting across from me in my own living room. He was a magnet for those seeking to find ways to bring peace and focus to their complicated lives. Both his reputation and his physical stature dwarfed the piece of furniture on which he sat.

My friend Michael Moran felt that Basil and I should meet. It was November of 1982, and Basil was speaking in Washington, DC, as part of a conference presented by the Shalem Institute for Spiritual Formation. I, along with more than 300 others, attended one of the presentations by Basil in the chapel at Trinity College. He was speaking on, or shall I say radiating, the joys of Centering Prayer. Of course, he did not want any of us to leave that day without experiencing the effects of such blessings.

Having been raised in the Episcopal Church, having attended an Episcopal-related college, and now having finished my seminary degree and been ordained a priest, I was not unaccustomed to prayer. I had been on more than one silent retreat and had spent time alone and in groups for quiet contemplation. Yet, I still recall sitting in that chapel as Basil invited us all to spend ten minutes in Centering Prayer, ending with the Lord's Prayer. Did I actually fall asleep, or did I simply come close to the edge? Heavens, did I snore? Centering Prayer is not one of my strongest gifts.

Later that day at home, there I was sitting across from this living monument to the power of prayer. A mix of awe, contrition, and bewilderment crowded my thoughts. Basil had heard from Michael about my vocation as a priest in starting the Center for

Liturgy and the Arts in 1981 as a nonprofit, freelance, peripatetic, itinerant ministry in the arts and worship. Through workshops, retreats, conferences, and such, I travel the country to teach others in music, drama, dance, clowning, juggling, storytelling, visual arts, and more. As Basil seemed to find his greatest bliss in stillness, I seemed to find mine in motion. What was emerging to connect us was that we had different approaches to the same goal: the experience of oneness with God.

By the end of our conversation, Basil was speaking about how we might meet in the future. The twenth-fifth anniversary of his ordination would be coming in December, at the abbey in Spencer, Massachusetts. Would I consider being there to offer a dance as part of his silver jubilee celebration? I would have to think about it, I said. It was definitely an honor, as well as a delight, but I had two unspoken hesitations. I suspected it would be a challenge financially. (Remember: artist, freelance, non-profit.) I was also a bit surprised that upon our first meeting, Basil would invite me to participate in such a major, personal event. I said I would contact him.

I wrestled briefly with the ideas of finances and appropriateness. I realized the first was about me and my own lack of trust in the heavenly economy. I conceded: all should be well, eventually. (Twenty-five years later, that mantra still proves helpful.) The idea of appropriateness was more about Basil, I discovered, and something I found challenging at other times with him.

I took some time to consider the possibilities of various pieces I had worked on already. I decided on two that I could offer, not knowing what exactly Basil had in mind. Though live music, spoken word, or even silence is usually preferred over recorded music, I expected I needed to be mostly self-sufficient in this case. If the abbey could amplify a cassette tape of recorded music, that would be the way to go. There was a piece called "Quiet Times," a recording of solo voice and piano performed by its composer, another priest Phillip Bennett. The other piece I thought I could offer was what I called "The Dance of the Lame Man," the story of Peter and John at the temple and their encounter with the lame beggar. The musical storytelling of this is part of a recording by Ken Medema called "People of the Son."

I called Basil. I told him I could think of two possibilities, but I thought it would be helpful if he told me a little more about what he had in mind and where in the celebration the dance might be used. He said, "I would like to have something in the quiet time after communion." I said, "I think I have exactly what you are looking for." After hearing the title and a bit about the piece, he agreed. Joyfully stunned that this collaboration across the miles was becoming clarified, I offered to tell him about the other piece, just in case another option might be helpful. When he heard about the story of Peter and John and the lame man, he responded immediately that there were people in his life who were Peter and John to him and who had helped him to stand. This piece would be appropriate at the reception following the Eucharist, where others would be giving testimonials about him. Basil wanted this dance to be his response at the end.

After arriving at the abbey, I had an opportunity to work with one of the monks, who would be my sound crew, and to rehearse the piece in the abbey church. This being Advent, there was a huge Advent wreath hanging over the center aisle in the midst of the choir. I told the monk that the cue for beginning the tape would be that I would walk out into the aisle and stand under the wreath, take a moment to center myself, and then he could push the button on the tape player.

After Mass was over, word reached me of some excitement that was narrowly averted. There was a local fellow who worked as a security guard and also frequently attended Mass at the abbey. He was thinking to himself how all sorts of folks show up at the abbey and he anticipated that one day some disturbed person would show up, and he wondered how he would respond. Before I (and he) knew it, there I was, walking barefoot into the center aisle. He was literally on the verge of tackling me, I was told later, when he noticed the monk poised at the tape player. The security guard decided to relax.

Nevertheless, there were some other repercussions. Apparently the dance was the subject of conversation in the sunroom with the monks between Mass and the reception. I had not thought to inquire, and Basil had not happened to mention that this was the very first time anyone had ever danced in the abbey church. The flip side of Basil's invitation to me turned out to be an invitation in another way to his own community to join in the celebration. I became a bit anxious as to what the monks might say (or not say) to me. Father Owen, a monk with white hair and two hearing aids, approached me to say, "Oh, Father, do you do that everywhere? That is the first time I have ever seen anything like that. That was wonderful!" I treasure that testimony to this day as a reminder of the joy that can come from remaining open to the new and unfamiliar as long as we live.

The second piece, slated for the end of the reception time in the Chapter Room, was danced from the point of view of the beggar. It began with the beggar sitting and leaning, in this case, on the door frame at the top of the stairs leading down into the room. I was dressed in what I consider a fairly abstracted version of tattered rags and shrouded with an old wool blanket. Apparently not abstracted enough. Some folks speculated that I was a vagrant that Basil knew and had invited. Appropriateness had multiple meanings in this case, all of which happened to work.

Years passed. Michael Moran moved about the country and eventually moved back to Washington, DC. His home became a gathering place on many occasions for visits with Basil. There were wonderful meals and times to share in Eucharist and prayer. Basil seemed to enjoy equally a Eucharist or a great meal. That is probably why he was a giant both in prayer and also in stature. He radiated joy and satiety after either the earthly or the heavenly meal, though there was usually a slightly rosier glow after the earthly meal.

Sometimes I was invited to bring my guitar and lead some singing as part of the Eucharist. One story from Basil stands out in my mind. I have danced and sung portions of Paul Winter's "Earth Mass" and find Susan Osborn's vocal contributions to it quite stirring. I was privileged to witness the Paul Winter Consort in a performance of the "Earth Mass" at the National Shrine of the Immaculate Conception in Washington, DC, many years ago. Susan embodied the music she sang. The sound rose up from within her and moved among us. At some point after that, Basil and Susan met. I can only imagine the meeting of these two individuals. Basil, as evangelist of Centering Prayer, eventually got Susan to agree to doing Centering Prayer for ten minutes a day. Susan said she would do so, only if Basil included music whenever he said the Mass.

Basil, as you would know by now, moved around the world. His gifts of leadership, vision, insight, peacemaking, and presence were put to work in various places. Eventually he was called to be abbot at the Monastery of Our Lady of the Holy Spirit in Conyers, Georgia. Again he asked me to dance for the celebration, this time the abbatial blessing for his installation as abbot in September of 2000. Guess where no one else had ever danced before? Here we go again. The community, God bless them, were unfailingly cordial and helpful. I was told later by someone visiting from the area how wonderful it was for the bishop to have gotten a chance to see liturgical dance, and perhaps that would lead to a more friendly climate for further use of movement in worship throughout the diocese.

It was difficult to imagine Basil "in retirement." There was still too much to be done, too much to be written. For health and other reasons, it seemed somewhat comforting that he could reside once again at the abbey in Spencer. We were amazed at how the years had flown by. Having once rather offhandedly spoken of dancing at his fiftieth anniversary of ordination, we found it was now becoming a near possibility. Instead, the world, literally, came crashing in. For a man who had spent the better portion of his life as a monastic and a priest, traveling the world in the pursuit and proclamation of peace through prayer, to die as a result of an automobile accident, on the way to his doctor, near his monastery home, seemed all too harsh and inconceivable.

It happened that I was already scheduled to be a part of the staff for the conference celebrating the twenth-fifth anniversary year of the Interim Ministries Network to be held in the Boston area that week of June 2005. The conference ended Thursday. The burial was scheduled for Friday. I was to be in Trenton, New Jersey, for the ordination of deacons on Saturday. My car was at the airport in Baltimore. All the details eventually worked out, including rebooking the airline ticket, within a very small window of possibilities. There would be space for me in the guesthouse across the road from the monastery in Spencer. I got a lift from my conference partner in liturgy planning who was headed in that direction.

Michael had already arrived and assisted in the arrangements for my stay. Abbot Francis Michael of Conyers, Abbot Damian of Spencer, and Brother Jude (who originally facilitated the introduction of Michael to Basil so many years ago) joined us for the evening at the monastery guest cottage. Over a lovely meal they provided for us, we shared the evening hearing and telling stories of Basil. Later in the stillness of the abbey church where Basil's body lay in repose, Michael and I took our turn at keeping watch by night. In the massive church, the body of one "larger than life" was yet not diminished.

The following day the Easter Liturgy was celebrated and Basil was returned to God's care, his body to the earth in the monastery cemetery. The visibly gathered community was simply a portion of those who joined that day in celebration of God's faithfulness as expressed in the life and work of M. Basil Pennington, ocso. The cloud of witnesses on that sunny day included all those throughout the world who have been encouraged to pray, to believe, and to journey on with enthusiasm and vigor in the manner of Dom Basil. He encouraged us to breathe deeply and to drink deeply of the wellspring of life. He demonstrated the way of delighting in what is seen and trusting in the mystery of what is unseen. A practical application of that simple way of living in delight and trust was the way that I was returned to the Boston airport by a vanload of inner city monastics I had met at the reception, who dropped me off on their way home.

I believe that Basil and I, in our different ways, share in the prayer to "Set us free, O God." For Basil, Centering Prayer was a way for people to be set free: to go to the place of quiet emptiness to discover what can be released, so that true freedom in Christ might be manifest in one's life. For me, it is the arts and in creating with others through which I pray that God will set us all free, that we may experience that abundant life God gives to us. The inner life and the outer life are partners in this journey. When this abundant life is present and manifest in us, as it was in Basil, we glow and radiate the glory of Christ. To that we all are witnesses.

Finally, while I am attempting to live an embodiment of prayer in motion, there are occasions when motion becomes simply action or activity, leading to exhaustion or discouragement (or maybe back surgery). The Shakers would remind us that our daily activity and action are the roots of our prayers: "Hands to work and hearts to God." Remembering Basil falling asleep upright at any hour of the day reminds me that getting tired out for God is not such a bad thing. Nevertheless, in those times when the stresses of daily life seek to defeat us, we are called back to our center, to the release from whatever holds us back from our fullness of life.

My left leg is stiff, my left foot is numb. It is difficult to walk, dance, or sing. All shall be well, eventually. Somewhere, during Advent in December of this year (2007), the golden jubilee of my brother Basil, I will find some way to dance in his honor and in thanksgiving for the many times our paths have crossed in this life. It would be appropriate. The candle has made it all through this day, and so have I. It is time to extinguish the candle. It is time to radiate from within. Thank you, Basil.

REFLECTION

Robert Goldschmidt

From the beginning, it was unique and improbable. My wife, Karen, and I met Basil when he came to Tarrytown, New York, to give a talk on Centering Prayer at our local parish. He was invited to come by John Sullivan, a former seminary classmate of his and a friend of ours.

During dinner at the Sullivans', Basil mentioned that he was on his way to the University of Notre Dame from which John and I were graduated. He was invited there by a sculptor to create some appropriate prose for a work depicting the Way of the Cross. We mentioned that our son Erik was a student there and wouldn't it be nice if they met. Small world. . . . Erik was a friend of the sculptor and actually was with him when Basil arrived. Basil and Erik became close friends. How I enjoyed each of our many, many conversations and the depths to which they went.

Cardinal Egan, who spent some time with Basil in Rome, shared with me that he thought Basil was one of the most intelligent men he had ever met, yet Basil never made a point of flaunting it. I remember our marvelous conversations over four-hour lunches when Basil would return to New York twice annually from his monastery in Hong Kong; his installation as abbot of the Monastery of the Holy Spirit in Georgia; his story of the reply the monks received from the Department of Agriculture regarding the soil sample they had sent asking what kind of crops it could support . . . "bricks"; the beauty of his Mass on our patio; the joy of celebrating the fiftieth anniversary of his ordination; his great address to the attendees at the annual Diocesan Fiscal Managers Conference in DC; his presence; his joy; his love; his fire.

I miss him terribly.

Fully Present

Casy Padilla

I met Father Basil well over a decade ago when he was my mother's houseguest at our home in the Philippines. They were planting the seeds of what would eventually become Contemplative Outreach Philippines. My encounter then was nothing more than the formality of an introduction. He even may have returned a second or third time as our houseguest, but as my mother planned a hectic calendar for him during his visits, we only managed brief hellos. Little did I realize then how he was to figure in a very personal and ongoing process of healing.

I moved to the United States in March of 1998. It was, in hindsight, a very hasty decision. As it turned out, it was also the best decision I ever made. I had been quite unhappy for a number of years, and they had taken their toll on my state of mind.

One day when my mom was visiting, she asked if I would drive her to Spencer, Massachusetts, so she could visit with Father Basil, and perhaps I could also talk with him. Having been a few months into my therapy, I had taken to discussing with my mom the various concepts I had been exposed to in my sessions. I also enjoyed driving around New England, so it sounded like a wonderful way to spend the day. Looking back, I had no expectations for that day apart from a beautiful drive, a nice conversation with my mother, and a pleasant time with her and Father Basil.

This was to be my first extensive encounter with Father Basil. After pleasantries and fairly light conversation over lunch, my mom purposely left us to chat. At first, I didn't talk about anything particularly sensitive about myself. Although we had met before, he wasn't a confidante by any stretch of the imagination. But there was a quality—not only about him, but also about the time he spent with me—that soon made me at ease sharing more personal information about myself. It went beyond my talking and his listening. I simply call it his presence. For the entire time I had the conversation with him, I felt I had his complete attention. He didn't seem to be concerned with anything other than listening to what I had to say. I, and no one else, was his concern at that time. Nothing else was as important as what I had to say, and he wanted to hear it, all of it. He never glanced at his watch, nor looked distantly to show any hint of impatience or boredom. I told my mom about the encounter, and she said, "That's just Father Basil living in the present!"

My second and, unfortunately, my last encounter with Father Basil was on another visit to Spencer the year before Father Basil passed away. Again, we had lunch at his favorite Spencer restaurant. This time, though, he invited us back to the abbey. My mom left us again to talk, and he said we could chat in his office. I felt so privileged, because he took me to parts of the abbey restricted to outside visitors. I had a personal guided tour. In his office, we talked about a lot of things. This time I felt I could tell him anything, and it was incredibly easy to open up to him. He put me at such ease. Not once did I ever feel a hint of any personal judgments injected into the conversation. It didn't escape me that this was only my second extensive encounter with Father Basil, and yet he treated me (and I certainly felt) as if he had known me for years. Again, I felt it—his absolute, attentive presence.

Over time, I have begun to understand what I believe Father Basil wanted to impart to me. In my case, he wasn't a teacher who educated with words. I was educated by his very actions—

his demeanor, his attentiveness, his complete focus on me and whatever I had to say to him. My mom had always talked about "letting go," which I took to mean forgetting the hurts I had in the past and trying to move on. I learned a different kind of letting go from Father Basil. He let go of everything! When I was with him, I felt that nothing pressed on him—nothing in the past, and nothing in the future. He let go of every concern he had to be present with you and you alone for that particular time. What entered my mind was the picture of a true saint—man who emanates love because he values everything about you like he values no other. What is beautiful about him is that I know I am not unique in having this experience with him. In two relatively brief but beautiful encounters with Father Basil, I learned that to love purely is to be fully present to each and every individual with whom you engage.

News of his accident and death came as a shock. Mom asked if we could drive up to Spencer for his funeral Mass and burial. She didn't have to ask. It was the least I could do for such a blessed individual. Normally it would take about an hour from where we were to get to Spencer, and we timed our departure to arrive thirty minutes before the funeral Mass began. Heading up I-91 to get to the Massachusetts Turnpike, we ran into an unusual amount of slow-moving traffic. The delay ate into the extra time allowance, and eventually into the Mass time itself. I remember asking my mom if she just wanted to turn back and visit on another day, but she gently insisted on continuing on our journey to Spencer. By the time we had arrived at St. Joseph's Abbey two-and-a-half hours after we started the journey, the funeral Mass should have been over for about an hour. However, cars still lined the sides of the road leading to the abbey church.

As I got to the rotary in front of the church, to my surprise there was a single available space to park. And an even bigger surprise, the funeral Mass was not yet over! As my mom and I entered the chapel through the side door, the monks were just about to proceed to the grounds at the back for Father Basil's burial. My mom, teary-eyed, whispered her good-byes to Father Basil and wished she could actually witness the burial rites. One of the monks turned in our direction and motioned for us to follow him. It was such a cathartic moment for my mother to be able to see Father Basil to his final resting place and to be able to express her good-byes in her own manner. We love to think that Father Basil, fully present even in death, postponed meeting his maker for just one more hour, so that a few dear friends could properly express their good-byes.

For What Am I Thankful?

Michael Moran

On a beautiful August afternoon in 1978, I drove up the long and winding tree-lined driveway to St. Joseph's Abbey in Spencer, Massachusetts. I had come seeking information about Centering Prayer. I had only just heard of Centering Prayer and arrived at the abbey under the impression that it was a new way of praying developed by Father Basil Pennington. Centering Prayer was of interest to me because in the fall semester of graduate school, at the Catholic University of America, I was scheduled to take a course in the theology of prayer. I thought if I could find out something about it, I'd be better prepared for the course.

I rang the bell to the beautiful stone building that serves as the monastery guesthouse. Brother Jude answered the door, thus becoming the first of many Trappist monks I would eventually come to know. After his gracious welcome, I told him why I was there. To my surprise, he offered to see if Father Basil could meet with me and invited me to wait in one of the reception rooms. A few minutes later, the doorway to the room was filled with a giant of a man with inviting blue eyes and an enormous white beard, dressed in the black and white habit of a Trappist monk with no socks and black Birkenstock sandals. I immediately felt at ease in his gentle and inviting presence and explained what had brought me to the abbey.

Not far into that first conversation, Father Basil offered to teach me Centering Prayer. He said it was quite simple—"Just close your eyes, sit relaxed and quiet and be in faith and love to God who dwells in the center of your being. If any thought comes to mind, just let it go." He went on to say, "You might choose a word like *Jesus* or *love* and when you become aware of anything, anything at all, simply, gently return to the Lord with the use of that prayer word." Off we both went into what turned out to be twenty minutes of complete and peaceful silence. At the end of the twenty minutes, I heard Basil, very softly and slowly, begin to recite the Our Father. After the experience, we had a long discussion about Centering Prayer. Eventually I came to know one of Basil's favorite axioms, "Experience first, discuss later."

I asked if there was a way one could have a brief experience of Trappist life. Basil immediately invited me to spend the night in a cottage, within the enclosure of the monastery. So began a twenty-eight-year friendship during which there always seemed to be in my schedule a trip to where he was or in his schedule a trip to where I was.

According to ancient monastic tradition, when Robert Pennington joined the Trappists in 1951, another name was given to him. It was Aloysius. In an article he wrote some years later, Basil explained that "happily about a year later another Aloysius appeared on the scene, one of the few survivors of the Trappist monastery in Northern China, and that gave them one Aloysius too many." He was then given the opportunity to choose another name. He chose Basil because Basil was the only saint named in the Rule of St. Benedict. In addition, he took Mary as his first name in religion. This is not a requirement but rather a choice available to Trappist monks. He had a deep devotion to the Blessed Mother and signed his name M. Basil Pennington, ocso. The M was an abbreviation for Mary; ocso is the acronym for the Latin title Cistercian Order of the Strict Observance. Only later, Basil said, as he came to know the spiritual teachings of Basil the Great, did he appreciate how providential his choice was.

According to Donald Attwater's *The Penguin Dictionary of Saints*, St. Basil the Great was born into an old Christian family of wealth and distinction. He was educated and formed a deep friendship with St. Gregory of Nazianzus. When St. Basil was twenty-seven years of age, he visited the chief monastic centers of the East and his influence was vast in the monastic life of the Orthodox Church. As a bishop, he was involved in difficult relations with the pope, St. Damasus. Valens, the Arian emperor, feared him, and sought to diminish his authority by administrative measures. Attwater goes on to say of St. Basil that he set a very high value on friendship and had a strong practical sympathy for the poor and downtrodden. A great deal of what is known about his life is derived from his own letters and sermons, which give a vivid picture of his many-sided character and activities.

The man who became Basil Pennington trod an amazingly similar path. Robert Pennington was born into a devout Christian family, was well-educated and formed deep friendships, and certainly had a strong practical sympathy for the poor and downtrodden.

Like Basil the Great, Basil Pennington visited monastic centers in the East and even came to live for almost four months in 1976 on Mount Athos. His extended visit there is documented in detail in *The Monks of Mount Athos: A Western Monk's Extraordinary Spiritual Journey on Eastern Holy Ground*. He eventually became biritual—that is, he was authorized to celebrate the Eucharist in both the Byzantine and the Roman rites—and created a Byzantine Chapel at St. Joseph's Abbey. As with Basil the Great, Basil Pennington dealt with the challenge of living under authority in his monastic career, and we know much about this thinking and many-sided character and activities from his letters and writings.

Basil also was deeply influenced by St. Francis de Sales. In an e-mail written to friends in 2005, he said, "It was in a retreat under the guidance of St. Francis de Sales in the fall of 1950 that I discerned my contemplative vocation and decided to follow it. . . . St. Francis had a deep passionate love for Jesus and this motivated his deep love for everyone else and his great dedication to the work of the Church. Working where Francis did he had to be ecumenical but he never watered down the teaching of the Church nor his loyalty to the Holy Father. He was certainly a man of prayer."

Whenever one spent a day with Basil, it would always include the celebration of Mass and at least two twenty-minute periods of Centering Prayer, one of which often occurred after receiving the Eucharist during Mass. Mass also would most often include a shared homily, with Basil saying after the readings, "What do you hear the Lord saying to us today?" At the end of Mass, participants would enter into the rest of the day having experienced divine abundance during an encounter with God at the center of their being during Centering Prayer and in readings from Scripture and a shared homily. Basil's experience of divine abundance during Centering Prayer and *lectio divina* seemed to be the context in which he then experienced and partook of divine abundance in all aspects of life.

St. Francis de Sales talks about the affinity between God and man and how it consists above all in what he beautifully describes as "the most sweet and agreeable meeting of abundance and indulgence. In other words, God's infinite riches, and man's poverty, complement each other and tend toward each other, in order to be united and interlocked. The divine superabundance fills human insufficiency to overflowing." I believe these ideas of St. Francis de Sales explain why Basil lead such a productive life, why he related to life the way he did, and how he made a difference in the lives of so many people all over the world.

In the *Treatise on the Love of God*, St. Francis de Sales says, "The sun's rays give light while giving warmth and warmth while giving light. Inspiration is a heavenly ray that brings into our hearts a warm light that makes us see the good and fires us on to its pursuit." During almost three decades of knowing Basil, the one thing that seemed to be his major focus was to share with as many people as possible a way to access those heavenly rays. He did this through letters, e-mails, books and articles, workshops on Centering Prayer and *lectio divina*, and the gift of his presence, while living for extended periods of time at four different monasteries, as a professor of theology, spirituality, and canon law, vocation father, trouble shooter, superior and abbot. In addition, along with John Sommerfeldt, Basil started the Institute of Cistercian Studies and Cistercian Publications at Western Michigan University, through which the rich literary resources of the Cistercian-Trappist tradition were translated into English and made available to the church at large.

For four years, Basil was responsible for men who came to St. Joseph's Abbey to discern if they were being called to the monastic life. He would meet with them after the evening meal and discuss some aspect of monastic life. These men encouraged him to transform these talks into a book. These requests resulted in an Episcopal priest, Father Win Lewis, and myself going off with Basil in 1982 to Nantucket, Massachusetts, to write *A Place Apart*. In the morning Basil would write a chapter for the book while Win and I went jogging, and in the afternoon we would review what he had written while Basil went for a swim. Over the evening meal, Win and I would share our ideas on the chapter that sometimes led to additions or revisions. Basil looked for ways to involve others in what he was up to in life and seemed to identify, acknowledge, and call forth gifts and competencies in others they often had not yet identified within themselves.

In May of 1988, I rendezvoused with Basil in Israel for a two-week visit to the Holy Land. On the first few nights in Tel Aviv, we stayed at the home of a Jewish couple Abraham and Yael Katzir. Basil was working with Yael on a book they were co-authoring on St. Bernard of Clairvaux. The book was to honor St. Bernard on the nine-hundredth anniversary of his birth in 1090. Yael was just one of many people who would co-author a book with Basil.

That trip to Israel eventually resulted in another book, *Journey in a Holy Land: A Spiritual Journal*, published in 2006 after Basil's death. He had not had time to edit the journal he kept during our visit to Israel until he retired at Spencer in May 2002. The manuscript for the book was at the publishers in March 2005 when the automobile accident occurred that led to his death sixty-seven days later on the feast of the Sacred Heart.

Over the years, I witnessed Basil delivering many workshops. He would start them by picking up *The Jerusalem Bible* he always had with him, and saying, "Now a word from my sponsor." Then he would read a passage and relate it to prayer. He would say a little bit about Centering Prayer or *lectio divina* followed by having the participants center or read something from Scripture. After a designated period of time, he'd have everyone share with a partner what happened while they centered or engaged in *lectio divina*. Then he would invite people to share what they had experienced with the entire group. He always focused those present on sharing what the experience was like for them and not what they thought about the experience. The majority of the workshop would be comprised of a conversation between Basil and the participants on what they had experienced and in responding to their questions.

Basil was open to being elected the abbot of a monastery, and on August 4, 2000, at the age of sixty-nine, he was elected abbot by the community at Our Lady of the Holy Spirit Monastery in Conyers, Georgia. He served in that capacity for twenty-one months until resigning on May 12, 2002. While at Conyers, he celebrated his seventieth birthday and the fiftieth anniversary of his entrance into the religious life.

During his time at Conyers, the invitations to attend meetings and to conduct Centering Prayer and *lectio divina* workshops kept coming in—some he accepted and some he declined. After being invited to do a workshop in England in 2001, he said in an e-mail, "Like it or not I am going to have to slow down a good bit or I'll never last for five years here, so I better not attempt England this year."

In a statement issued at the time of his resignation from the abbacy at Conyers, he said he had helped the community through its transition and felt it was time for the fifty monks he led to choose an abbot from among themselves, adding in his letter of resignation: "All the days of my life and into eternity, I will hold each of the men of this community in a very special love and prayer."

Two years later, Father Francis Michael Stiteler, who had served as Abbot Basil's prior, was elected to lead the community. After resigning as the abbot on May 12, 2002, Basil returned to St. Joseph's Abbey, the monastery he had entered in 1951.

Basil's retirement was full, but not as full as before. He continued to write books and meet with guests at Spencer Abbey. On July 26, 2002, he celebrated the golden jubilee of his monastic profession with many of his family and friends followed by a period of time in one of the hermitages on the grounds of the abbey, where he spent his seventy-first birthday in solitude.

In November of that year, his Uncle Charley died. Basil was unable to go to the funeral, but in one of his weekly articles he reflected on the influence his uncle had had on his life, suggesting, "We older men might ask ourselves, how well are we positioned to be an accessible listening ear for the young men of today?"— something at which he was a master.

In January 2004, Basil wrote, saying: "The days seem to be taken up being with folks—and that is good. I hope to bring joy and peace, hope and encouragement—Jesus to each one." At the beginning of Lent, he wrote: "For one thing, I'm going to be very faithful to my workouts three times a week, and my daily walk. Being as fully alive as we can be and letting the Lord work in and through us is one way we can hasten the coming of the kingdom." On Valentine's day, he wrote: "I finished my book with Ratner's drawings on Wednesday night and met my publisher on Thursday to turn it over to him. Now I have nothing under contract. Free at last. After I went to enjoy a couple hours with Harvey Cox and William Sloane Coffin. We reminisced about the good old days."

After Lent, he wrote: "It has been a good Lent and the days ahead look very full and blessed. I now have several books in the works, each with a collaborator or publisher, which I like, but no contracts so no push. Life is very full and there are quiet hours with the Lord that make it all so spacious." In addition, he had accepted an invitation from the Abbot General to work on a literary history of the order for the last century.

In April, he hosted a meeting of the International Thomas Merton Society's New England group and represented the Spencer community at a subsequent meeting at St. Anselm's Abbey, Manchester, New Hampshire. He spent two weeks of August with his brother Tom and his family in Alabama and Florida. In November, he hosted what turned out to be his last meeting with the Ecumenical Institute of Spirituality (EIOS). Many thought it was one of the best ever meetings and Basil added, "It opened out to infinite possibilities: interfaith, lots of new members, e-group (if you want to join: EIOS-subscribe@yahoogroups.com), offshoots in the West, etc. Deo Gratias."

In early May, I visited Basil for what turned out to be the last time we were together. We enjoyed long walks in the woods, dinners out, and visits with friends. After spending what he described as a great week at Conyers, where he attended the abbatial blessing of his successor, he returned to Spencer and spent his seventy-second birthday in solitude, again in one of the monastery's hermitages.

As is the case for thousands of people throughout the world, Basil has had and continues to have an enormous influence on my life, on how I show up in the world and how the world shows up for me. He kept showing up in my life for almost thirty years, and every time he did, I got back on track with the spiritual practices of *lectio divina* and Centering Prayer.

I miss being able to communicate with him via e-mails, phone calls, and visits. I miss being able to dine and travel with him. I miss seeing him doing laps in the swimming pool. I miss centering and talking about the Scriptures with him. I miss watching him deliver workshops. But on the other hand, he is with me every day—especially during *lectio divina* and Centering Prayer.

The article he wrote at Thanksgiving 2004 and e-mailed to friends is a beautiful description and benediction of his life, of the spirit with which he lived and shared it, and of the gift he was and is to all of us.

For what am I thankful? Truth to tell I expect to spend all eternity in thanksgiving and still not complete the joyous task. I thank God for being God and being our

God, so loving and so near, so full of love and care. We are singularly blessed in knowing God, even if this knowledge leaves us with a multitude of questions and challenges.

And can we never thank God enough for the gift of each other, for giving us each other? And can we thank each other enough for being the gift we are to each other? Yes, our loved ones and all those who have and do nurture us, but also all those who share this planet with us and make human life and culture possible. We don't all do a very good job of that but, thank God, we do it well enough so that we continue and each day grow more conscious of what we have to do so it will continue.

I can start a litany: I thank God for sun and sky, for moon so full, for fresh air and cooling breezes, for flowers and trees and the Canada geese and all their winged friends. I thank God for wide-eyed children who challenge me to see and wise old ones who call me to wisdom. I thank God for the friend I can hold in my arms, with whom I can share the laughter and on whose shoulder I can shed my tears.

I thank God for this beautiful abbey, for all the monks here, for the friends who come and pray and praise with us, for all those who help us to continue here.

I thank God . . . (I will leave it to you to go from here. And as you do, please thank God for me.)

Abba Basil

And so I do thank God for Basil, and so do thousands of others, every day.

About the Contributors

Arnold Mark Belzer is the rabbi of Congregation Mickve Israel in Savannah, Georgia, the third-oldest Jewish congregation in the United States. He is one of the founders of the Mastery Foundation and vice president of its Board of Trustees.

David G. Benner is a psychologist, retreat leader, and the author of more than twenty books. He is Distinguished Professor of Psychology and Spirituality at Psychological Studies Institute in Atlanta and Distinguished Author in Residence at Carey Theological College in Vancouver, Canada.

Stephen J. Boccuzzi is a senior scientist and tenured health services researcher with a diversity of clinical and research experience. He is currently involved in health policy research for a major health care informatics and consulting company in Pennsylvania.

Werner Erhard is an educator, consultant, and the creator of one of the most influential technologies of the last thirty years, the technology of transformation. This technology has been the basis for two popular and effective educational programs, The est Training and The Landmark Forum, as well as several other enterprises and organizations.

Lewis S. Fiorelli, OSFS, is a former superior general of the Oblates of St. Francis de Sales. He has taught and written extensively on Salesian spirituality and served as a retreat director and spiritual guide to many individuals, both lay and religious.

Matthew Flynn, OCSO, entered St. Joseph's Abbey in Spencer, Massachusetts, six months after Basil Pennington. They studied together at St. Joseph's abbey and also for a year in Rome. Most of Father Matthew's ministry has been in the retreat house at Spencer.

Laurence Freeman, OSB, is a Benedictine monk of the Congregation of Monte Oliveto and the Director of The World Community for Christian Meditation (www.wccm.org). He is the author of *Jesus, the Teacher Within.*

Erik P. Goldschmidt is a doctoral student in counseling psychology at Boston College. He has been a high school English teacher, a graduate student of theology, a liturgical musician, and writer of folk music.

Robert Goldschmidt was chief financial officer for a publicly traded company and a private equity firm. After his retirement, he served for eight years as chief financial officer for the Catholic Archdiocese of New York. He currently serves on the board of two companies and three community organizations.

E. Glenn Hinson is the recently retired professor of spirituality and John Loftis Professor of Church History at Baptist Theological Seminary at Richmond, Virginia, and the author of twenty-seven books. Currently, he serves as visiting professor of church history at Candler School of Theology at Emory University in Atlanta, Georgia.

Thomas Keating, OCSO is by all accounts the most important American Trappist of the last century. He was Dom Basil's abbot at St. Joseph's Abbey; he is the founder of Contemplative Outreach Ltd., the author of many books, and lives at St. Benedict's Monastery in Snowmass, Colorado.

Martha F. Krieg is a senior programmer/analyst for a computer firm and translates Cistercian books into English. She is in formation as a lay associate of New Melleray Abbey.

Megan Lange is an owner, with her husband, Robert, of Robert Lange Studios, a fine art gallery in Charleston, South Carolina.

Robert Lange is a painter, artist, and grandnephew of Basil Pennington. With his wife, Megan, he is owner of Robert Lange Studios.

Elias Marechal, ocso, is novice director at Holy Spirit Monastery in Conyers, Georgia. Before entering the monastery, he was a teacher of Transcendental Meditation and was able to contribute some of that experience to the development of the practice of Centering Prayer.

Michael Moran is a board member of the Mastery Foundation, assistant superior general of the Sons of St. Francis de Sales, and a member of the leadership team for his parish church in London. He retired from the United States Navy in 1998 after a thirty-year career as a commissioned officer and registered nurse.

Karol O'Connor, osb, is a member of the Benedictine Community at Kylemore Abbey in County Galway, Ireland, where she teaches music in the International Boarding School and is choir mistress in the community.

Gerry O'Rourke is a priest and former head of the Office of Ecumenical and Inter-religious Affairs for the Catholic Archdiocese of San Francisco. He is also one of the founders of the Mastery Foundation and the current chairman of the Board of Trustees.

Ann Overton is the executive director and a founder of the Mastery Foundation, one of several organizations Basil Pennington was instrumental in creating, as well as an educator, writer, and editor.

Casy Padilla is the son of Grace Padilla and a student in the allied health field at a college in Connecticut.

Grace Padilla is a secular Franciscan and a national board member of the Catholic Women's League in the Philippines. She helped organize and establish the Philippine chapter of Contemplative Outreach and continues to teach and promote Centering Prayer.

Cynthia Pennington is married to Neil, one of Father Basil's nephews. They live in Charlotte, North Carolina, with their three children, Jacqueline, Carter, and Victoria.

Jasper Pennington is a retired priest of the Episcopal Diocese of Michigan and archivist of the Pennington Research Association housed at Earlham College in Richmond, Indiana.

Franck Perrier is the founder and chief executive officer of Eyeka, a new company dedicated to creating an online community of user-generated photography and video. Previously, he was chief executive officer of Corbis France, a global image agency.

Armand Proulx is the pastor of Second Congregational Church in Greenfield, Massachusetts, and a former member of the LaSalette Missionaries. He conducts Centering Prayer workshops throughout the United States.

Mark Scott, OCSO, entered the Abbey of Our Lady of New Clairvaux in Vina, California, in 1978. Early in 2000, Father Mark accepted Father Basil's invitation to help out at Assumption Abbey in Ava, Missouri. He was elected as Ava's fifth abbot in December of 2001.

John Sommerfeldt is professor of history at the University of Dallas. He was the founding director of the Medieval Institute and Institute of Cistercian Studies at Western Michigan University, where he was the progenitor of the Cistercian Studies Conference. He is the author or editor of twenty-six books.

Bruce Stewart is founding director of the Center for Liturgy and the Arts, an adjunct faculty member in the oral interpretation of Scripture at Virginia Theological Seminary and liturgical dance at Wesley Theological Seminary. He is also chaplain at Goodwin House Alexandria, a continuing-care retirement community.

Francis Michael Stiteler, OCSO, entered the Monastery of the Holy Spirit in Conyers, Georgia, in July of 1974. He has served over the years as junior and novice master and was elected the monastery's seventh abbot in May of 2004.

Theophane Young, OCSO, now a monk of Our Lady of Joy Abbey in Hong Kong, entered the Spencer monastery in 1988, after careers in education and UN refugee work in Asia. He is now on special mission teaching English in mainland China.

Basil Pennington's personal icon of St. Basil the Great

Appendix

BASIL'S THREE CORE TEACHINGS AND SPIRITUAL PRACTICES

Reprinted with permission from *Centered Living: The Way of Centering Prayer*, M. Basil Pennington, OCSO, Liguori, MO: Liguori/Triumph, 1999.

Guidelines for Centering Prayer

M. Basil Pennington, OCSO

Sit comfortably in a chair that will give your back good support and gently close your eyes. It is well to choose a place where you will not be disturbed by any sudden intrusion. A quiet place is helpful, though not essential.

Sit relaxed and quiet.

1. Be in faith and love to God who dwells in the center of your being.

2. Take up a love word and let it be gently present, supporting your being to God in faith-filled love.

3. Whenever you become aware of anything, simply, gently return to the center with the use of your prayer word.

At the end of twenty minutes, let the Our Father (or some other prayer) pray itself.

Guidelines for *Lectio Divina*

M. Basil Pennington, OCSO

It is well to keep the sacred Scriptures enthroned in our home in a place of honor as a real Presence of the Word in our midst.

1. Take the Sacred Text with reverence, acknowledging God's Presence, and call upon the Holy Spirit.

2. For five minutes (or longer if you are so drawn), listen to the Lord speaking to you through the Text and respond.

3. At the end of the time, choose a word or phrase (perhaps one will have been given to you) to take with you and thank the Lord for being with you and speaking to you.

IMPORTANT DATES IN THE LIFE OF BASIL PENNINGTON

1928 November 11, Parents are married

1929 September 28, Birth of older brother, Dale

1931 July 28, Robert John Pennington (Basil) born in Brooklyn, New York

1936 June 2, Birth of younger brother, Tom

1938 December 8, His father, Dale Kelsey Pennington, dies at the age of thirty-three

1951 June 18, Enters St. Joseph's Abbey, Spencer, Massachusetts

1953 July 26, Simple Profession on the feast of St. Anne

1956 September 8, Solemn Profession

1957 December 21, Ordained to the priesthood

1958–60 Earns a licentiate in Sacred Theology from the Angelicum in Rome

1962 Returns to Rome and earns a licentiate in Canon Law

1962–65   Assisted at the Second Vatican Council as a peritus for Bishop Mulroney of Brooklyn and in the preparation of the new Code of Canon Law

1967   Chosen as a member of the Law Commission of the Trappist order

1968   Initiated the translation of the Cistercian Fathers into English. Plans for Cistercian Publications accepted by the American Region of Cistercian Superiors

1971   Pope Paul VI asks Trappists to do what they can to help the church redefine its contemplative dimension

1972   Institute established (now the International Congress on Medieval Studies) at Western Michigan University, Kalamazoo, Michigan

1973   Centering Prayer movement begins

1976   May 31, Departs for three-and-a-half-month visit to Mount Athos. Establishment of the Institute of Cistercian Studies, including Cistercian Publications and a Cistercian library at Western Michigan University

1980   August 10, His mother, Helene Josephine Kenny Pennington, dies at the age of seventy-five

August 14–September 27, Visit to India

1981   December 21, Celebrates twenty-fifth anniversary of ordination to the priesthood

1983   Collaborates with an interfaith group to establish the Mastery Foundation

1984   Along with Werner Erhard leads the first Mastery Foundation program *Making a Difference: A Course for Those Who Minister*

1986–89   Accepts Dom Flavian Burns's invitation to help out at Assumption Abbey in Ava, Missouri

1987   May 19–June 6, Visit to Israel

1991–98   Assists at Our Lady of Joy Monastery, Lantau Island, Hong Kong, serving as right-hand man to the superior, novice master, and junior master

1998   Trip to monasteries in Kenya and Uganda

2000   February 14, Returns to Assumption Abbey, Ava, Missouri, as *superior ad nutum*, at the invitation of Dom Brendan Freeman, abbot of new Melleray Abbey, Prosta, Iowa

   August 4, Elected as sixth abbot of Our Lady of the Holy Spirit Monastery, Conyers, Georgia

   September 8, Abbatial blessing at our Lady of the Holy Spirit Monastery

2002   May 12, Resigns as abbot of Our Lady of the Holy Spirit Monastery and returns to St. Joseph's Abbey, Spencer, Massachusetts

2003 July 26, Golden Jubilee of monastic profession

2005 March 29, Sustains numerous injuries in a serious automobile accident near St. Joseph's Abbey while driving to a medical clinic

June 3, Dies in a hospital in Worcester, Massachusetts, as a result of injuries sustained in March 29 automobile accident

June 10, Funeral and burial at St. Joseph's Abbey, Spencer, Massachusetts

Abbey—A monastic community governed by an abbot.

Abbot—The priest who is head of an abbey, generally elected by the monks. A monastery must have been granted the status of an abbey by the pope. Abbot and Dom are used interchangeably. Dom is short for the Latin term of address *domne* ("lord") given to Benedictine priests in France and England in the Middle Ages.

Apophatic—Theology based on saying what something is by saying what it is not.

Canon law—The body of laws and regulations governing the Catholic Church.

Cenobite—A member of a communal religious order.

Choir—Generally that part of the church where the stalls of the clergy are.

Cistercians—Religious of the Order of Cîteaux, a Benedictine reform order established in 1098 for the purpose of restoring as far as possible the literal observance of the Rule of St. Benedict. Today they are divided into three bodies: the Common Observance, the Middle Observance, and the Strict Observance (Trappists).

Divine office—Also known as the Liturgy of the Hours, the prayers or psalms appointed to be sung at eight different hours throughout the day.

Dom—See abbot.

Ecumenical—Concerning the promotion of unity and cooperation among worldwide Christian churches.

Eremite—The name for early Christians who retired from society to devote themselves to spirituality.

Eucharist—The celebration and reenactment of the last supper Christ had with his disciples; same as Mass.

Hermit—One who lives in seclusion.

Incunabula—Editions of the Bible issued before the year 1500.

Laity/lay persons—Refers to those who are faithful but are not ordained as clergy.

Lectio divina—Latin for divine or spiritual reading, a method of prayer incorporating scriptural reading.

Liturgy—The form of worship or ritual practiced by a religious group.

Mass—The celebration and reenactment of the last supper Christ had with his disciples; same as Eucharist.

Mass crypt—An underground chamber where Mass is said.

Novice—A person admitted into a religious order in preparation for the profession of permanent vows.

Novitiate—The period of preparation for religious life after completion of a postulancy.

OCSO—Ordo Cisterciensis Strictioris Observantiae; Cistercians Order of the Strict Observance [OCSO/Trappists]. The order began as a reform movement at the Abbey of Notre Dame de la Grande Trappe in 1664 in reaction to the relaxation of practices in many Cistercian Monasteries. The Trappists take their informal name from La Trappe.

Peritus—(Latin for "expert") The title given to Roman Catholic theologians present to give advice at an ecumenical council.

Postulant—A candidate for religious profession or holy orders; postulancy is the probationary stage before the novitiate.

Prior—A monastic superior, usually lower in rank than an abbot; in Trappist monasteries, the assistant to the abbot.

Profession—The public declaration of religious vows.

Superior ad nutum—An appointed, interim superior (*ad nutum*—at the nod).

Thurible—Covered incense burner, generally suspended on a chain so it can be carried in procession.

Trappists—See entry at OCSO.

Vespers—The evening prayer of the divine office.

Bibliography of Books Written by M. Basil Pennington, OCSO

Compiled by Martha F. Krieg

Abbey Prayer Book. Selected and arranged by M. Basil Pennington. Liguori, MO: Liguori/Triumph, 2002.

Aelred of Rievaulx: The Way of Friendship: Selected Spiritual Writings. Edited by M. Basil Pennington. Hyde Park, NY: New City Press, 2001.

Awake in the Spirit: A Personal Handbook of Prayer. New York: Crossroad, 1992.

Bernard of Clairvaux: A Lover Teaching the Way of Love. Hyde Park, NY: New City Press, 1997.

Bernard of Clairvaux: A Saint's Life in Word and Image. By M. Basil Pennington, Yael Katzer, and Ned Johnson. Huntington, IN: Our Sunday Visitor, 1994.

The Bread of God: Nurturing a Eucharistic Imagination. By Tony Kelly and M. Basil Pennington. Liguori, MO: Liguori Publications, 2001.

Breaking Bread: The Table Talk of Jesus. San Francisco: Harper & Row, 1986.

Call to the Center: The Gospel's Invitation to Deeper Prayer. 3rd ed. Hyde Park, NY: New City Press, 2003. (First edition Garden City, NY: Doubleday, 1990; second edition Hyde Park, NY: New City Press, 1995.)

Called: New Thinking on Christian Vocation. New York: Seabury, 1983.

A Centered Life: A Practical Course on Centering Prayer. Kansas City, MO: Credence Cassettes, 1994.

Centered Living: The Way of Centering Prayer. Liguori, MO: Liguori, 1999. (Previous edition Garden City, NY: Doubleday, 1986.)

Centering Prayer: In Daily Life and Ministry. By Thomas Keating, OCSO, and M. Basil Pennington. New York: Continuum, 1998.

Centering Prayer: Renewing an Ancient Christian Prayer Form. Garden City, NY: Image Books, 1980, Image Reprint edition 1982.

Challenges in Prayer. Liguori, MO: Liguori Publications, 2005.

The Christ Chaplain: The Way to a Deeper, More Effective Hospital Ministry. By Robert John Pennington. Binghamton, NY: Haworth Pastoral Press, 2007.

Circling to the Center: One Woman's Encounter with Silent Prayer. By Susan M. Tiberghien and M. Basil Pennington. Mahwah, NJ: Paulist Press, 2001.

The Cistercians. Collegeville, MN: Liturgical Press, 1992.

Cottage Talks: Monastic Spirituality for Active Christians. Kansas City, MO: Credence Cassettes, 1984.

Daily We Follow Him: Learning Discipleship from Peter. Garden City, NY: Image Books, 1987. (Previously published as *In Peter's Footsteps*. Garden City, NY: Doubleday, 1985.)

Daily We Touch Him: Practical Religious Experiences. Kansas City: Sheed & Ward, 1997.

Engaging Scripture: Reading the Bible with Early Friends. By Michael L. Birkel and M. Basil Pennington. Richmond, IN: Friends United Press, 2005.

Engaging the World with Merton: On Retreat in Tom's Hermitage. Brewster, MA: Paraclete Press, 2005. (Previously published as *On Retreat with Thomas Merton.*)

Eucharist: Wine of Faith, Bread of Life. Revised ed. Liguori, MO: Liguori/Triumph, 2000.

The Eucharist Yesterday and Today. New York: Crossroad, 1984.

The Fifteen Mysteries: In Image and Word. Illustrated by William Hart McNichols. Huntington, IN: Our Sunday Visitor, 1993.

Finding Grace at the Center: The Beginning of Centering Prayer. By Abbot Thomas Keating, OCSO, M. Basil Pennington, OCSO, and Thomas E. Clarke, SJ. Woodstock, VT: SkyLight Paths Publishing, 2007. (Previously published as *Finding Grace at the Center: The Beginning of Centering Prayer.* Still River, MA: St. Bede Publications, 1978.)

Gift of Being Yourself: The Sacred Call to Self-Discovery. By David G. Benner and Basil Pennington. Downer's Grove, IL: InterVarsity Press, 2004.

Helen! Then Shall You Truly Dance: Helen's Story. By Helen Chase and M. Basil Pennington. Makati City: GOSPA Foundation, Republic of the Philippines, n.d.

I Have Seen What I Was Looking For: Thomas Merton. Edited by M. Basil Pennington. Hyde Park, NY: New City Press, 2005.

In Peter's Footsteps: Learning to Be a Disciple. Garden City, NY: Doubleday, 1985.

In Search of True Wisdom: Visits to Eastern Spiritual Fathers. New York: Alba House, 1995.

An Invitation to Centering Prayer. Liguori, MO: Liguori/ Triumph, 2001.

Journey in a Holy Land: A Spiritual Journey. Brewster, MA: Paraclete Press, 2006.

Jubilee: A Monk's Journal. New York: Paulist Press, 1981.

Lectio Divina: Renewing the Ancient Practice of Praying the Scriptures. New York: Crossroad, 1998.

Lessons from the Monastery that Touch Your Life. New York: Paulist Press, 1994.

Light from the Cloister: Monastic Prayer and Practice for Everyone. New York: Paulist Press, 1991. (Previously published as *A Place Apart*.)

Like Father Like Son: Bernard of Clairvaux and Thomas Merton. In John R. Sommerfeldt [ed], Bernardus Magister: Papers Presented at the Nonacentenary Celebration of the Birth of Saint Bernard of Clairvaux (CS-135, 1992).

Listen with Your Heart: Spiritual Living with the Rule of Saint Benedict. By M. Basil Pennington and Chaminade Crabtree. Brewster, MA: Paraclete, 2007.

Listening: God's Word for Today. New York: Continuum, 2000.

Living in the Question: Meditations in the Style of Lectio Divina. New York: Continuum, 1999.

Light from the Cloister: Monastic Prayer and Practice for Everyone. New York: Paulist Press, 1991. (Previously published as *A Place Apart*.)

Living Our Priesthood Today. By M. Basil Pennington and Carl Arico. Huntington, IN: Our Sunday Visitor, 1987.

The Living Testament: The Essential Writings of Christianity since the Bible. New York: HarperCollins, 1985.

Long on the Journey: The Reflections of a Pilgrim. Huntington, IN: Our Sunday Visitor, 1989.

The Manual of Life: The New Testament for Daily Reading. New York: Paulist Press, 1985.

Mary Today: Challenging Woman, Model for Maturing Christians. Garden City, NY: Doubleday, 1989.

Monastery: Prayer, Work, Community. San Francisco: Harper & Row, 1983.

Monastic Journey to India. New York: Seabury, 1982.

Monastic Life: A Short History of Monasticism and Its Spirit. Petersham, MA: St. Bede's Publications, 1989.

The Monastic Way. New York: Crossroad, 1990.

The Monks of Mount Athos: A Western Monk's Extraordinary Spiritual Journey on Eastern Holy Ground. Woodstock, VT: Skylight Paths Publications, 2003. (Previously published as *O Holy Mountain! Journal of a Retreat on Mount Athos*. Garden City, NY: Doubleday, 1978.)

A Place Apart: Monastic Prayer and Practice for Everyone. Garden City, NY: Doubleday, 1983.

Place Apart Series I: Monastic Prayer and Practice for Everyone. Liguori, MO: Liguori/Triumph, 1998. (See also *A Place Apart*, 1983.)

Pocket Book of Prayers. Selected with an introduction. Garden City, NY: Image Books, 1986.

Poetry as Prayer: The Psalms. Artwork by Helen Kita. Boston: Pauline Books & Media, 2001.

Pray Attention. By M. Basil Pennington and Michael Mauney. U.S. Catholic. Digital. July 28, 2005.

Prayer and Liberation: The Ecumenical Institute of Spirituality. Edited by M. Basil Pennington. Canfield, OH: Alba Books, 1976.

Prayer Times: Morning–Midday–Evening. A Pocket "Liturgy of the Hours" for All Christians. Garden City, NY: Image Books, 1987.

Praying by Hand: Rediscovering the Rosary as a Way of Prayer. San Francisco: HarperSanFrancisco, 1991.

Psalms: A Spiritual Commentary. Illustrated by Philip Ratner. Woodstock, VT: SkyLight Paths Publishing, 2006.

A Retreat with Thomas Merton. Warwick, NY: Amity House, 1988.

Rule and Life: An Interdisciplinary Symposium. Edited by M. Basil Pennington. Shannon, Ireland: Irish University Press, 1971.

Saint Bernard of Clairvaux: Studies Commemorating the Eighth Century of His Canonization. Edited by M. Basil Pennington. Kalamazoo, MI: Cistercian Publications, 1977.

A School of Love: The Cistercian Way to Holiness. Harrisburg, PA: Morehouse, 2001.

Seeking His Mind: 40 Meetings with Christ. Brewster, MA: Paraclete Press, 2002.

So, What's the Go(o)d Word for Today? New York: Continuum, 2000.

The Song of Songs: A Spiritual Commentary. Woodstock, VT: SkyLight Paths Publishing, 2004.

Thomas Merton: I Have Seen What I Was Looking For: Selected Spiritual Writings. By Thomas Merton. Edited by M. Basil Pennington. Hyde Park, NY: New City Press, 2005.

Thomas Merton, Brother Monk: The Quest for True Freedom. New York: Continuum, 1997. (Previous edition: San Francisco: Harper & Row, 1987.)

Thomas Merton, My Brother: His Journey to Freedom, Compassion and Final Integration. Hyde Park, NY: New City Press, 1996.

Through the Year with the Saints: A Daily Companion for Private or Liturgical Prayer. New York: Image Books, 1988.

Toward an Integrated Humanity: Thomas Merton's Journey. Edited by M. Basil Pennington. Kalamazoo, MI: Cistercian Publications, 1988.

True-Self/False-Self: Unmasking the Spirit Within. New York: Crossroad, 2000.

Twentieth Century Martyrs of the Cistercian Order of the Strict Observance: Martyrs of Algeria, Martyrs of the Spanish Civil War, Martyrs of the Chinese Communists: Their Story. Spencer, MA: St. Joseph's Abbey, 1997.

20 Mysteries of the Rosary: A Spiritual Journey. Liguori, MO: Liguori Publications, 2003.

Vatican II: We've Only Just Begun. New York: Crossroad, 1994.

The Way Back Home: An Introduction to Centering Prayer. New York: Paulist Press, 1989.

Who Do You Say I Am? Meditations on Jesus' Questions in the Gospel. Hyde Park, NY: New City Press, 2005.

William of St. Thierry: The Way to Divine Union: Selected Spiritual Writings. Edited by M. Basil Pennington. Hyde Park, NY: New City Press, 1998.

Wisdom for the Journey: Conversations with Spiritual Fathers of the Christian East. Edited by Basil Pennington and Serge Bolshakoff. Staten Island, NY: Alba House, 2001.

Bibliography of Scholarly Books Written by M. Basil Pennington, OCSO

Compiled by Martha F. Krieg

An incomplete list that does not include his many scholarly articles.

Aelred of Rievaulx: The Liturgical Sermons. The First Clairvaux Collection. Translated by Theodore Berkeley and M. Basil Pennington. Kalamazoo, MI: Cistercian Publications, 2001.

The Cistercian Spirit: A Symposium in Memory of Thomas Merton. Edited by M. Basil Pennington. Kalamazoo, MI: Cistercian Publications, 1973.

Contemplative Community: An Interdisciplinary Symposium. Edited by M. Basil Pennington. Washington, DC: Cistercian Publications, 1972.

Last of the Fathers: The Cistercian Fathers of the Twelfth Century: A Collection of Essays. Still River, MA: St. Bede Publications, 1983.

One Yet Two: Monastic Tradition East and West. Edited by M. Basil Pennington. Cistercian Studies Series 29. Kalamazoo, MI: Cistercian Publications, 1976.

Word and Spirit: Saint Bernard of Clairvaux (1090–1153). By Michael Casey, Jean Leclercq, and M. Basil Pennington. Still River, MA: St. Bede Publications, 1990.